FAMILY
COOKBOOK

BHS

Contents

Introduction
page 6

Meals for Two
pages 7-13

Family Meals
pages 14-23

Quick Meals
pages 24-31

The Family Roast
pages 32-35

Vegetables
pages 36-43

Meals with Salads
pages 44-51

Meals without Meat
pages 52-55

Meals for Special Occasions
pages 56-63

Index
page 64

Introduction

Being married, having looked after a family for a number of years and having worked for a long time as a professional cook, I felt there was a gap in the market for a cook book that would give well-balanced, nourishing meals for a growing family, without stretching the pocket too far.

In this book I have tried to provide a variety of recipes, as it is easy to get tied to a weekly routine of Sunday is chicken, Monday is stew, and so on, and then having your family tell you what day it is by what's on their plates.

There are times, of course, when you only have the two of you to cater for and, therefore, you can celebrate with a special meal, so I have included some extra special recipes that I hope you will find a joy to prepare and eat.

Always remember that presentation is a major part of any meal, and take time over this, setting a table to complement your meal. I have also included some of the more traditional recipes that, in this day and age of convenience foods, may have been forgotten.

This book, I hope, will help you enjoy cooking for your family, as opposed to just filling a gap when they are hungry.

Smoked Haddock in
French Mustard Sauce (top),
Chicken Curry (left) and
Poussin in White Sauce (right).

Meals for Two

Poussin in White Sauce

1 pkt sage and onion stuffing
2 poussins
Fat
300ml (½ pint) milk
25g (1oz) plain flour
25g (1oz) soft margarine
Salt and pepper

Make the stuffing as directed on the packet and use to stuff the poussins. Place the poussins in a roasting tin with melted fat, and cook in the oven for 30-40 minutes at 180°C, 350°F, Gas Mark 4, until tender. Put the milk, flour, margarine and seasoning into a pan and bring gradually to the boil, whisking all the time. Cook gently for 3 minutes, stirring. Serve with baked potatoes and sweet corn with red peppers.
Serves two.

Smoked Haddock in French Mustard Sauce

350g (¾lb) smoked haddock fillet, skinned and cut into two
A little milk
Salt and pepper
15g (½oz) butter
15g (½oz) flour
150ml (¼ pint) milk
15ml (1 tblsp) French mustard
Chopped chives (optional)

Place the fish in an ovenproof serving dish. Pour a little milk over the fish and season. Cover and

cook in the oven for 15-20 minutes at 160°C, 325°F, Gas Mark 3. Heat the butter in a pan, stir in the flour and cook for 2 minutes. Allow to cool, then pour in the milk gradually. Bring to the boil, stirring. Season and stir in the French mustard. Spoon the sauce over the fish and garnish with chopped chives if desired. Serve with potato croquettes and broccoli.
Serves two.

Mixed Grill

2 sausages
Liver
2 pork chops
Tomatoes
Mushrooms, sliced if flat

Grill the sausages, liver, pork chop and tomatoes until tender. Boil mushrooms until soft. Serve with baby new potatoes.
Serves two.

Chicken Curry

25g (1oz) butter
1 small chicken, jointed
1 small onion, peeled and chopped
1 small apple, peeled and chopped
5ml (1 tsp) curry powder
10g (¼oz) flour
2.5ml (½ tsp) curry paste
300ml (½ pint) chicken stock
1 chilli (optional)
Pinch of powdered ginger
Pinch of powdered turmeric
5ml (1 tsp) chutney
Squeeze of lemon juice
Salt and pepper
25g (1oz) desiccated coconut
15g (½oz) sultanas

Garnish
Thin onion rings, lightly fried
Thin green pepper rings, lightly fried
Lemon rind, lightly fried

Heat the butter and fry the chicken pieces. Remove and drain on paper towels. Fry the onion and apple for 2-3 minutes, then add the curry powder, flour and curry paste. Cook briefly, then carefully blend in most of the stock, reserving 50ml (2 fl oz). Bring to the boil and cook for a few minutes until a thin sauce. Add the remaining spices, chutney, lemon juice and seasoning. Return the chicken pieces to the pan. Pour the remaining stock over the coconut

and allow to stand for a few minutes, then add the strained liquid to the curry. If preferred, fresh coconut or coconut milk can be used instead. Add the sultanas then cover and simmer for 2-3 hours. Garnish with onion, pepper and lemon rind to serve.
Serves two.

Plaited Lamb

450g (1lb) minced lamb
2 onions, peeled and chopped
25g (1oz) breadcrumbs
15g (1 tsp) dried rosemary
15ml (1 tblsp) tomato purée
15ml (1 tblsp) Worcestershire sauce
2 eggs, beaten
Salt and pepper
225g (8oz) puff pastry

Mix together the minced lamb, onions, breadcrumbs, rosemary, tomato purée, Worcestershire sauce and one of the eggs. Add salt and pepper. Roll out the pastry on a floured surface into an oblong. Place the lamb mixture in the centre, cut diagonal strips from the centre to the edges along both sides. Brush all four sides with a little beaten egg. Fold the pastry at each end and then fold the strips over alternately so they meet in the centre. Place the plaited lamb on a greased baking tray and brush with the remaining beaten egg. Cook in the oven for 15-20 minutes at 220°C, 425°F, Gas Mark 7. Then reduce the heat to 180°C, 350°F, Gas Mark 4 and cook for a further 30 minutes. Serve with new potatoes and a green vegetable.
Serves two.

Pasta Fish Pie

40g (1½oz) macaroni
Salt
225g (8oz) white fish

Cheese Sauce
15g (½oz) butter or margarine
15g (½oz) flour
150ml (¼ pint) milk
Salt and pepper
Pinch of dry mustard
40g (1½oz) Cheddar cheese, grated

Break the macaroni into small pieces (if using long macaroni) and cook in 2 pints of boiling, salted water until tender. Meanwhile, simmer the fish in a little salted water until tender. Lift the fish out

and flake with a fork. Heat the butter or margarine in a pan, stir in the flour, and cook the 'roux' for 2-3 minutes over a low heat. Remove the pan from the heat and gradually add the milk, seasoning and mustard. Bring to the boil, cook until thickened, then add the grated cheese. Put the drained macaroni and fish into a hot dish and top with the cheese sauce. Place for 2-3 minutes under a hot grill until the cheese topping bubbles. Serve with runner beans and sweet corn.
Serves two.

Braised Beef

15g (½oz) fat
350g (12oz) of brisket or topside of beef cut into pieces
1 carrot, peeled and sliced
1 onion, peeled and sliced
1 turnip, peeled and sliced
1 leek, trimmed and sliced
2 sticks celery, trimmed and sliced
25g (1oz) fat bacon, diced
Bouquet garni (mixture of fresh herbs, i.e. parsley, thyme, sage, in muslin bag)
Salt and pepper
150ml (¼ pint) beef stock
60ml (2 fl oz) red wine

Heat the fat in a flameproof casserole or large saucepan and brown the meat for 3 minutes. Lift the meat onto a plate. Brown the vegetables in the fat together with the diced bacon. Add the bouquet garni, seasoning, stock and wine then return the meat on top of the mixture. Cover tightly and cook very slowly for about 1 hour. Lift the lid from time to time and add more stock if the mixture appears to be running dry. Remove the bouquet garni. Sieve the vegetables and stock to make a sauce or use a blender and reheat with the meat. Serve with boiled potatoes.
Serves two.

Stuffed Mushrooms

Two large, flat mushrooms
15g (½oz) butter
1 rasher of streaky bacon, rinded and chopped
15g (½oz) fresh breadcrumbs
5ml (1 tsp) chopped parsley
Grated rind of ¼ lemon
2.5ml (½ tsp) lemon juice
25g (1oz) Cheddar cheese, grated
Salt and pepper
Cress

Remove the stalks from the mushrooms and chop finely. Heat the butter and fry the mushroom stalks and the bacon for a few minutes. Remove from the heat and stir in the breadcrumbs, parsley, lemon rind and juice, and cheese. Season well. Place the mushroom caps on a greased baking sheet, divide the filling between each cap and cook for 15-20 minutes at 170°C, 325°F, Gas Mark 3. Sprinkle with cress. Serve with sweet corn and sauté potatoes.
Serves two.

Veal Cutlets Bonne Femme

2x225g (two 8oz) veal cutlets
Salt and pepper
25g (1oz) flour
50g (2oz) clarified butter or butter and oil mixed
100g (4oz) boiled, cold potatoes, thinly sliced
50g (2oz) button onions
50ml (2 fl oz) sherry
150ml (¼ pint) demi-glacé sauce
15ml (1 tblsp) chopped parsley

Sprinkle the veal cutlets with salt and pepper and dredge with flour. Heat the butter or butter and oil, in a frying pan and gently fry the cutlets on both sides for a few minutes. Place the cutlets in an ovenproof dish and cook in the oven for 15-20 minutes at 180°C, 350°F, Gas Mark 4 until tender. Fry the potatoes in the same pan until golden brown, remove and keep warm. Fry the onions for two minutes. Transfer the onions to a saucepan of water and boil until soft. Drain off the butter and pour the sherry into the pan. Add the demi-glacé sauce and bring to the boil, stirring continuously. Arrange the cutlets on a serving dish, surrounded by the fried potatoes and onions. Cover with the demi-glacé sauce and decorate with chopped parsley.
Serves two.

Facing page: Plaited Lamb (top left), Pasta Fish Pie (top right) and Veal Cutlets Bonne Femme (bottom).

Bacon and Chestnuts

450g (1lb) joint of bacon, boned and rolled
25g (1oz) butter
1 small onion, peeled and chopped
50g (2oz) chestnut purée
1.25ml (¼ tsp) mixed herbs
1.25ml (¼ tsp) mixed spice
5ml (1 tsp) soft brown sugar
1 beaten egg
450g (1lb) puff pastry

Place the bacon in a saucepan, cover with cold water, bring to the boil then simmer for 1 hour. Remove the bacon from the pan and trim off any excess fat, leave until cold. Melt the butter and fry the onion until soft. Mix with the chestnut purée, herbs, spice and sugar, and half the beaten egg to bind the mixture. Roll out the pastry to a circle large enough to wrap around the bacon joint. Spread the mixture over the top of the bacon. Fold the pastry up over the joint and seal with a little of the beaten egg. Place on a baking sheet. Brush with beaten egg. Cook in the oven for 30-35 minutes at 220°C, 425°F, Gas Mark 7. Serve with carrots and broad beans.
Serves two.

Demi-Glacé Sauce

25g (1oz) dripping or butter
25g (1oz) peeled and chopped onion
25g (1oz) peeled and chopped carrot
25g (1oz) flour
1 rasher bacon, rinded and diced
600ml (1 pint) brown stock
5ml (1 tsp) tomato purée
5ml (1 tsp) mixed herbs
Salt and pepper

Heat the dripping or butter, fry the onion, bacon and carrot until very lightly browned. Do not overcook at this stage as burnt onion gives a bitter taste to the sauce. Add the flour and continue cooking slowly until a rich chestnut colour. Draw

This page: Braised Beef (top left), Mixed Grill (centre) and Stuffed Mushrooms (bottom).

Facing page: Filled Jacket Potatoes (top left), Sausage and Mushroom Pie (top right), Bacon and Chestnuts (bottom right) and Stuffed Aubergines (bottom left).

Pork Fillets and Apricots

225g (8oz) pork fillet, cut into small pieces
15ml (1 tblsp) seasoned flour
25g (1oz) butter
200g (7oz) can of apricot halves
15ml (1 tblsp) Worcestershire sauce
15ml (1 tblsp) soft brown sugar
10ml (2 tsp) wine vinegar
5ml (1 tsp) lemon juice
2.5ml (½ tsp) powdered cinnamon
60ml (4 tblsp) water
100g (4oz) long grain rice

Toss the pork pieces in the seasoned flour. Heat the butter in a flameproof casserole and fry the pork until lightly browned. Chop all but three of the apricot halves. Mix 4 tablespoons of the apricot syrup with the Worcestershire sauce, sugar, vinegar, lemon juice, cinnamon and water. Pour the apricot sauce and chopped fruit over the pork. Bring to the boil, stirring continuously. Reduce the heat, cover and simmer for 15 minutes. Meanwhile, cook the rice in boiling, salted water. Spoon pork and sauce onto a serving dish and spoon the drained rice around the meat. Decorate with the reserved apricots. If required serve with a green vegetable.
Serves two.

the pan aside, add the stock and when all the liquid has been incorporated, add the purée, herbs and seasoning to taste. Bring to the boil, skim thoroughly and simmer, covered, for 30 minutes. Strain through a fine-meshed strainer, pressing as much as possible of the vegetables through.
Makes 1 pint.

Sausage and Mushroom Pie

225g (8oz) pork sausages
25g (1oz) butter
1 onion, peeled and sliced
20g (¾oz) flour
150ml (¼ pint) milk
150ml (¼ pint) brown stock
Salt and pepper
Pinch of mixed herbs
100g (4oz) sliced button mushrooms
225g (8oz) puff pastry
1 egg, beaten

Prick the sausages and grill them until golden. Heat the butter in a pan and fry the onion for 5 minutes. Stir in the flour and cook for a further minute. Gradually add the milk and stock and bring to boil. Stir until thickened then add the seasoning, herbs and mushrooms. Place the sausages in a pie dish and pour over the mushroom sauce. Roll out the puff pastry, and use to cover the dish. Trim off any excess pastry. Glaze the top of the pie with the beaten egg and cook in the oven for 40 minutes at 200°C, 390°F, Gas Mark 6. Serve with new or boiled potatoes and a green vegetable.
Serves two.

Stuffed Aubergines

3 medium aubergines, washed and stalks removed
Salt
275g (10oz) butter
1 medium onion, peeled and finely chopped
1 clove garlic, peeled and crushed
175g (6oz) minced beef
400g (14oz) can of tomatoes
15ml (1 tblsp) chopped parsley
5ml (1 tsp) dried marjoram
10ml (2 tsp) tomato purée
Pepper
10ml (2 tsp) cornflour
100g (4oz) Cheddar cheese, grated

Slice the aubergines in half lengthways. Scoop out the flesh carefully and chop finely. Put the flesh on a large plate, sprinkle with salt and leave for 30 minutes. Blanch the aubergine skins in boiling water for 5 minutes. Remove and place on a serving dish. Heat the butter, add the onion and garlic and cook until soft. Stir in the minced beef and cook until brown. Add the tomatoes, parsley, marjoram and tomato purée. Season with pepper and bring to the boil. Blend the cornflour with a little cold water and add to the beef and tomato mixture. Return to the boil, then remove from the heat. Drain the aubergine flesh in a sieve and rinse in cold water. Stir half the flesh into the beef and tomato mixture and use to stuff the aubergine halves. Top each one with grated cheese and cook in the oven for about 30 minutes at 180°C, 350°F, Gas Mark 4. (Use the left-over aubergine flesh in a bolognese sauce or as a vegetable covered with a cheese sauce.) Serve the stuffed aubergines hot with a tossed green salad.
Serves two.

Hearts and Stuffing

2 lambs' hearts
Seasoned flour
20g (¾oz) unsalted butter
300ml (½ pint) brown stock
1 small onion
100g (4oz) carrots
1 celery heart

Stuffing
2 shallots
1 stick celery
25g (1oz) belly pork
25g (1oz) fresh breadcrumbs
1 rounded tblsp parsley
5ml (1 tsp) curry powder
Salt and pepper
20g (¾oz) melted butter

First make the stuffing. Peel and chop the shallots. Scrub and dice the celery stick. Mince or finely chop the pork. Place these ingredients in a bowl with the breadcrumbs, parsley, curry powder and seasoning. Bind together with the melted butter. Rinse the hearts. Cut out any tubes and discard, and fill the hearts with the stuffing. Sew up the openings and coat the hearts with seasoned flour. Melt the butter in a heavy pan and fry the hearts over a

high heat until brown. Lift the hearts into a casserole dish. Stir in enough seasoned flour to absorb the fat. Cook for 2-3 minutes then add the stock and bring to the boil. Pour over the hearts. Cover the casserole and cook in the oven at 170°C, 325°F, Gas Mark 3 for 2 hours. After 2 hours peel and chop the onion, carrot and celery heart. Add to the casserole and continue to cook for a further 1 hour. Serve with boiled potatoes and green vegetables.
Serves two.

Filled Jacket Potatoes

2 medium-sized potatoes
25g (1oz) butter
Salt and pepper

Cheddar Cheese Filling
75g (3oz) Cheddar cheese, grated
25g (1oz) butter
A little milk
Salt and pepper
15ml (1 tblsp) Parmesan cheese

Bacon Filling
75g (3oz) bacon, rind removed, chopped and fried
25g (1oz) butter
A little milk
Salt and pepper
1 small green pepper, cored, seeded and finely chopped

Sausage and Onion Filling
2 small pork sausages, chopped and grilled
25g (1oz) butter
A little milk
Salt and pepper
1 small onion, peeled, chopped and fried

Liver and Courgette Filling
75g (3oz) lamb's liver, chopped and fried
25g (1oz) butter
A little milk
Salt and pepper
2 small courgettes, diced and fried

Scrub the potatoes well. Prick them and dot their skins with butter. Sprinkle lightly with salt and pepper. Cook in the oven for 1-1¼ hours at 200°C, 400°F, Gas Mark 6. When cooked, cut in half lengthways and scoop out the centres, keeping the skins intact. Mash the potato in a basin, adding one of the filling mixtures. Return the mixture to the potato skins. Cook for a further 15-20 minutes.
Serves two.

Lasagne

150g (5oz) margarine
1 small onion, peeled and sliced
100g (4oz) minced beef
200g (7oz) can of tomatoes
5ml (1 tsp) tomato purée
150ml (¼ pint) beef stock
5ml (1 tsp) dried marjoram
5ml (1 tsp) mixed herbs
Pinch garlic salt
Salt and pepper
5ml (1 tsp) cornflour
75g (3oz) lasagne
10g (¼oz) butter
100g (4oz) margarine
150g (5oz) flour
150ml (¼ pint) milk
75g (3oz) Cheddar cheese, grated

Heat the margarine and fry the onion until soft. Stir in the minced beef and cook until browned. Add the tomatoes, tomato purée, stock, herbs and garlic. Season well, cover and simmer for 30 minutes. Meanwhile, mix the cornflour to a paste with a little cold water, stir into the meat sauce and bring to the boil, stirring continuously. Cook the lasagne in boiling, salted water, adding the 10g (¼oz) butter, for 10-15 minutes. Drain carefully. Heat the margarine, stir in the flour and cook for a few minutes. Allow to cool and gradually add the milk. Return to the heat and bring to the boil, stirring continuously. Stir in two-thirds of the cheese. Cover the base of a greased ovenproof dish with half the lasagne. Spoon over half the meat and tomato sauce. Cover with the remaining lasagne and spoon over remaining tomato sauce. Pour on the cheese sauce, sprinkle the Cheddar cheese on top and cook in the oven at 190°C, 375°F, Gas Mark 5 for 30-35 minutes.
Serves two.

Facing page: Lasagne (top left), Hearts and Stuffing (top right) and Pork Fillets and Apricots (bottom).

Family Meals

Cod in White Sauce

675g (1½lb) cod fillet
Salt and pepper
150ml (¼ pint) milk
30ml (2 tblsp) lemon juice
25g (1oz) butter

White Sauce
25g (1oz) margarine
25g (1oz) flour
Milk
Salt and pepper
Pinch of paprika

Wash and skin the fish and cut into four pieces. Place the fish in an ovenproof dish and season well. Pour the milk and lemon juice over the fish and dot with some of the butter. Cover the dish and cook for 20 minutes at 200°C, 400°F, Gas Mark 6. Melt the margarine and remaining butter in a pan, stir in the flour and cook for 1 minute. Drain the liquid from the fish and add enough milk to make up to 300ml (½ pint). Stir the liquid slowly into the roux, bring to the boil and cook for 1 minute, stirring continuously. Add seasoning and paprika. Serve with new potatoes and broccoli.
Serves four.

Beef Surprise

1 onion, peeled and chopped
40g (1½oz) fat
25g (1oz) flour
300ml (½ pint) brown stock
Pinch of mixed herbs
450g (1lb) minced beef
Salt and pepper

Cook the onion in the fat until transparent. Add the flour and cook for 5 minutes. Add the stock, bring to the boil and cook until the sauce thickens. Add the herbs, minced beef and seasoning. Stir continuously, cook until the meat is browned. Lower the heat and simmer gently for 1 hour, stirring frequently. Arrange on a hot dish. Garnish with tomatoes and creamed potatoes, and serve.
Serves four.

Chicken Pie

Pastry
225g (8oz) flour
Pinch of salt
50g (2oz) margarine
50g (2oz) lard
Beaten egg and milk mixed together
    to glaze top of pie

Chicken Sauce
150ml (¼ pint) milk
15g (½oz) margarine
15g (½oz) plain flour
Salt and pepper
225g (8oz) cooked chicken, chopped
45ml (3 tblsp) white wine (optional)

First make the sauce by placing the milk, margarine and flour in a small pan. Bring to the boil, whisking continuously. Simmer for 2 minutes until the sauce thickens. Add seasoning, stir in the chopped chicken and add the wine, if desired. Sift the flour and salt into a bowl and rub in the margarine and lard until it looks like breadcrumbs. Add enough water to form a dough. Use half the dough to line a large, flat plate. Add the chicken mixture then cover with the remaining pastry, sealing the edges. Cut slits in the top. Brush the top of the pie with the beaten egg and milk mixture. Cook in the oven for 25 minutes at 200°C, 400°F, Gas Mark 6 until golden brown. Serve with creamed potatoes and carrots.
Serves four.

Spaghetti Bolognese

25g (1oz) butter
15ml (1 tblsp) olive oil
50g (2oz) mushrooms, chopped
1 onion, peeled and chopped
1 carrot, peeled and chopped
225g (8oz) minced beef
100g (4oz) tomato purée
300ml (½ pint) brown stock
225g (8oz) spaghetti
Parmesan cheese, to serve

Heat the butter and oil in a pan and fry the mushrooms, onions and carrot. Stir in the meat, cook for a few minutes then add the tomato purée and stock and simmer gently. Cook for one hour, until the mixture thickens, stirring occasionally. Meanwhile, place the spaghetti in boiling, salted water and cook for 15 minutes. Drain. Serve together with the bolognese sauce and sprinkle with Parmesan cheese.
Serves four.

Beef Bake

675g (1½lb) stewing steak
25g (1oz) flour
Salt and pepper
25g (1oz) lard
2 onions, peeled and chopped
600ml (1 pint) brown stock
15ml (1 tblsp) tomato purée
45ml (3 tblsp) red wine (optional)
2 carrots, peeled and sliced
10ml (2 tsp) dried mixed herbs

Topping
50g (2oz) white breadcrumbs
50g (2oz) butter
225g (8oz) self-raising flour
5ml (1 tsp) salt
Pepper
5ml (1 tsp) garlic salt
5ml (1 tsp) Parmesan cheese
45ml (3 tblsp) oil
150ml (¼ pint) milk

Cut the meat into cubes and toss in seasoned flour. Melt the lard in a pan and fry the onions. Add the meat and fry for 5 minutes or until the meat is brown. Remove from the heat and blend in the stock, tomato purée and red wine. Add the carrots and herbs. Return to the heat and bring to the boil. Turn the mixture into an ovenproof dish, cover and cook in the oven for 2 hours at 170°C, 325°F, Gas Mark 3. Fry the breadcrumbs in the butter until golden brown, then lift out on to a plate. Sieve together the flour, salt, pepper, garlic salt and Parmesan cheese, add the oil and milk and gradually mix to a dough. Drop large spoonfuls of the dough into the fried breadcrumbs and roll into balls. Arrange on top of the meat mixture. Return the casserole uncovered to the oven and cook for a further hour, or until the top is golden brown. Serve with peas and new potatoes.
Serves four.

Sweet and Sour Pork Chops with Rice

4 large pork chops

Sauce
400g (14oz) can of tomatoes
1 large green pepper, cored, seeded
    and chopped
30ml (2 tblsp) cornflour
45ml (3 tblsp) wine vinegar
30ml (2 tblsp) brown sugar
30ml (2 tblsp) soy sauce
Salt and pepper

To make the sauce place the tomatoes and 150ml (¼ pint) of their juice in a saucepan and break down with a fork. Add the green pepper, bring to the boil and simmer for 10 minutes. Blend the cornflour and vinegar together to form a paste. Add the paste to the tomato mixture. Add the remaining sauce ingredients and cook for 15 minutes. Meanwhile, cook the pork chops under a moderately hot grill. Place the chops on a flat, flameproof serving dish and pour over the sauce. Place under a hot grill for 2-3 minutes to heat through.
Serves four.

Pork Chops with Brussels Sprouts and Sweet Corn (far left, top), Beef Surprise (far left, bottom) and Cod in White Sauce (left).

Pork Chops with Brussels Sprouts and Sweet Corn

75g (3oz) butter
1 large onion, peeled and chopped
450g (1lb) Brussels sprouts
100g (4oz) frozen sweet corn
4 pork chops (large)
5ml (1 tsp) salt
5ml (1 tsp) cayenne pepper
5ml (1 tsp) chopped parsley

Melt 25g (1oz) of butter in a saucepan. Add the chopped onion and fry lightly. Cook the Brussels sprouts in boiling, salted water for about 8 minutes until cooked but still firm. Also cook the sweet corn. Drain both vegetables. Melt 25g (1oz) of the butter and add the drained Brussels sprouts and sweet corn and cook very gently, shaking the pan frequently. Melt the remaining butter. Sprinkle the pork chops with the salt and the cayenne pepper and fry them in the butter over a medium heat for about 5-10 minutes on each side. Remove the chops to a serving dish. Add 2 tablespoons of water to the juices in the pan and bring to the boil, stirring continuously. Arrange the vegetables round the chops and pour over the sauce. Sprinkle with the chopped parsley and serve.
Serves four.

Chicken Casserole

25g (1oz) lard
100g (4oz) mushrooms, sliced
4 chicken joints
75g (3oz) flour
2 large carrots, peeled and sliced
1 potato, peeled and sliced
300ml (½ pint) chicken stock
300ml (½ pint) white wine
Salt and pepper
75g (3oz) peas

Melt half the lard, fry the mushrooms, then place them in an ovenproof dish. Coat the chicken in the flour and fry in the remaining lard until golden brown. Transfer to the ovenproof dish and add the sliced carrots and potato. Put the leftover flour in a pan, add the stock and wine, stirring all the time. Add the seasoning, bring to the boil and pour over the chicken and vegetables. Cover and cook in the oven for 1 hour 35 minutes at 180°C, 350°F, Gas Mark 4. Add

the peas 10 minutes before the end of the cooking time. Serve with new potatoes.
Serves four.

Shepherd's Pie

25g (1oz) fat
1 onion, peeled and chopped
50g (2oz) mushrooms, chopped
2 tomatoes, skinned and chopped
350g (12oz) cooked beef or lamb, minced
Pinch of mixed herbs
Salt and pepper
300ml (½ pint) brown stock
450g (1lb) mashed potato
50g (2oz) butter

Heat the fat and fry the onion for 3 minutes. Add the mushrooms and fry for another minute. Add the tomatoes and the meat and cook for 3 minutes. Stir in the herbs and seasoning and finally add the stock. Put the mixture into a pie dish and cover with the mashed potato. Dot small pieces of butter over the mashed potato. Cook in the oven for 30-40 minutes at 200°C, 400°F, Gas Mark 6 until the top is crisp and brown. Serve with peas and leeks.
Serves four.

This page: Beef Bake (top left), Chicken Casserole (top right) and Sweet and Sour Pork Chops with Rice (bottom).

Country Chicken

4 chicken legs
Butter for frying
2 onions, peeled and chopped
25g (1oz) cornflour
A little milk
150ml (5 fl oz) hot chicken stock
100g (4oz) peas
100g (4oz) sweet corn

Fry the chicken legs in butter to seal. Set aside to drain on paper towels. Fry the onions until tender but not brown. Transfer the chicken and onions to an ovenproof dish. Blend the cornflour with the milk. Add the chicken stock. Add the peas and sweet corn to the casserole and pour the chicken stock over the vegetables but do not completely cover chicken. Cook in the oven, uncovered, for 20-30 minutes at 190°C, 375°F, Gas Mark 5. Serve with boiled potatoes.
Serves four.

Liver With Oranges

350g (12oz) lamb's liver
25g (1oz) flour
Salt and pepper
Pinch of mustard
50g (2oz) butter
15ml (1 tblsp) olive oil
1 onion
5ml (1 tsp) garlic salt
2.5ml (½ tsp) brown ketchup sauce
150ml (¼ pint) brown stock
2 oranges, peeled and sliced, to garnish
Creamed potatoes, to serve

Trim the liver and cut into 3-4 slices. Season the flour with salt, pepper and the mustard. Dip the liver into the seasoned flour. Melt half the butter and 5ml (1 tsp) of oil. Fry the liver in the butter and oil, cooking each side for 2-3 minutes. Remove the liver to a warmed dish and keep hot. Add the remaining butter to the pan and cook the onion until soft. Add the garlic salt and brown sauce. Stir in the stock. Simmer until the mixture thickens and add extra seasoning if desired. Place the liver on a serving dish, pour over the sauce and garnish with slices of orange. Pipe creamed potatoes round to make a border. Serves four.

Beef and Dumplings

450-675g (1-1½lb) stewing steak
Salt and pepper
25g (1oz) flour or
15g (½oz) cornflour
25g (1oz) fat
900ml (1½ pints) brown stock
Pinch of mixed herbs
2 onions, peeled and chopped
4 carrots, peeled and sliced

Dumplings
100g (4oz) self-raising flour
Pinch of salt
50g (2oz) suet
Water to mix

Wipe the meat and cut into small pieces. Remove excess fat. Coat the meat in seasoned flour or cornflour and fry in the fat for a few minutes to seal. Add the stock, herbs and vegetables, bring to boiling point. Transfer to an ovenproof dish and cover. Cook in the oven for 2½ hours at 180°C, 350°F, Gas Mark 4. Meanwhile, make the dumplings. Sieve the flour and salt into a basin. Add the suet and blend with a knife. Stir in enough water to bind. The dumpling mixture should be just soft enough to form into balls. Divide into 8 portions and roll into balls with lightly floured hands. If necessary, thicken the casserole with extra cornflour or flour, blended with a little cold water. Twenty minutes before the end of the cooking time put the dumplings into the simmering liquid. Leave uncovered, unless there is plenty of space between the dumplings and the lid, to allow them to rise well. Serve with boiled potatoes.
Serves four-six.

Liver with Oranges (facing page), Beef and Dumplings (centre) and Country Chicken (left).

Toad in the Hole

225g (8oz) sausages (pork or beef)
15g (½oz) lard
100g (4oz) plain flour
2.5ml (½ level tsp) salt
Pinch of garlic salt
1 egg
300ml (½ pint) milk

Put the sausages into a large, shallow tin or dish. Add the lard and place in the oven at 220°C, 450°F, Gas Mark 7. Sieve the flour, salt and garlic salt into a bowl. Add the egg and a little milk and beat until smooth. Add the rest of the milk a little at a time, beating well, to make a batter. Pour the batter into the tin. Cook for 30-45 minutes. Serve with mixed vegetables and duchesse potatoes. Serves three.

Meat Loaf

2 slices of bread
450g (1lb) prime minced beef
1 onion, peeled and chopped
5ml (1 tsp) Worcestershire sauce
Salt and pepper
1 egg, beaten

Grate the bread or place in a blender to produce crumbs. Mix the mince, onion, Worcestershire sauce, salt and pepper and breadcrumbs. Add the egg and bind the mixture together. Put the mixture into a greased loaf tin and cover with greaseproof paper. Cook in the oven for 50-60 minutes at 200°C, 390°F, Gas Mark 6. When the meat loaf is cooked the juices should run clear when a skewer is inserted. Turn the loaf out onto a flat serving dish. Garnish with cooked vegetables such as carrots, runner beans, peas and Brussels sprouts. Serves four.

Black Pudding with Apple

450g (1lb) potatoes, peeled
3 large cooking apples
45ml (3 tblsp) oil
25g (1oz) butter
450g (1lb) black pudding, sliced
5ml (1 tsp) chopped parsley

Boil and mash the potatoes and keep them warm. Peel and core the apples and cut each one into 8

segments. Heat half the oil and all the butter in a pan. Add the apple, cover and cook for 5 minutes on a low heat. Drain and keep warm. In another pan heat the remaining oil and add the sliced black pudding. Fry on both sides until it is slightly crisp and heated through. Remove and drain. Place the mashed potato in the centre of a heated serving dish and surround it with alternate portions of black pudding and apple. Sprinkle the potato with the chopped parsley. Serve with a green vegetable and fresh tomatoes.
Serves four.

Wine Coated Ham

1kg (2lb) ham
Salt and pepper
225g (8oz) carrots, peeled and cut into sticks
225g (8oz) turnips, peeled and cut into sticks
225g (8oz) green beans
225g (8oz) frozen peas
15ml (1 tblsp) soft brown sugar
150ml (¼ pint) red wine
50g (2oz) butter

This page: Wine Coated Ham (top), Black Pudding with Apple (centre right), Gammon Rounds with Onion Sauce (bottom left).

Facing page: Steak and Kidney Pudding (top left), Crunchy Lamb Pie (top right), Meat Loaf (centre left) and Toad in the Hole (bottom right).

Cover the ham with cold water and soak for 4 hours, changing the water frequently. Place the ham in a large pan, cover with cold water and simmer for 40 minutes. Bring a large pan of salted water to the boil, add the vegetables and cook for about 10 minutes. When the vegetables are cooked drain them, rinse with cold water and drain them again. Lift the ham from the pan. Peel off the rind and place the ham in an ovenproof dish. Sprinkle the ham with sugar and place in the oven for 5 minutes at 190°C, 375°F, Gas Mark 5. Pour the wine over and return to the oven for 5 minutes, basting frequently. Melt the butter in a pan and add the drained vegetables, salt and pepper. Heat through, stirring

continuously. Place the ham on a large serving dish with the vegetables and serve with the sauce from the cooking. Serve with new potatoes if required.
Serves four.

Gammon Rounds in Onion Sauce

4 gammon rounds
3 onions, peeled and sliced
50g (2oz) butter or margarine
50g (2oz) flour
Salt and pepper
600ml (1 pint) milk

Grill the gammon rounds until tender. Boil the onions until soft, then drain. Melt the butter or margarine, remove from the heat and stir in the flour. Return to the heat and cook gently for a few minutes. Remove the pan from the heat and gradually stir in the milk. Bring to the boil and cook, stirring with a wooden spoon, until smooth. Season well. If any small lumps have formed whisk thoroughly. Stir in the boiled onions and serve with the gammon. Serve with potatoes in their jackets, and runner beans. Serves four.

Crunchy Lamb Pie

25g (1oz) margarine
1 onion, peeled and chopped
½ packet parsley sauce mix
150ml (¼ pint) milk
1 tblsp thin cream or top of the milk
175g (6oz) cold, cooked lamb, minced
½ packet instant potato
25g (1oz) Lancashire or Cheddar cheese, grated

Heat the margarine and fry the onion until soft. Make the parsley sauce as directed on the packet, using the milk, and stir in the cream, or top of the milk and the onion. Add the lamb to the sauce. Mix well and turn into a greased pie dish. Make the instant potato as directed on the packet and spread over the meat mixture. Sprinkle the cheese over the potato. Cook in the oven for 30 minutes at 200-220°C, 400-425°F, Gas Mark 6-7. Serve with a green vegetable or baked onions.
Serves two.

Steak and Kidney Pudding

675g (1½lb) stewing steak
2 lambs' kidneys
15ml (1 tblsp) flour
Salt and pepper
150ml (¼ pint) stock

Suet Crust Pastry
225g (8oz) self-raising flour
5ml (1 tsp) baking powder
2.5ml (½ tsp) of salt
A pinch of pepper
100g (4oz) shredded suet
150ml (¼ pint) water

To make the suet crust pastry, sift flour, baking powder and seasoning into a mixing basin. Add the suet and stir in enough water to mix to a firm dough. Turn out on to a floured board and use as required. Trim and cut the steak into strips. Cut the kidneys into small pieces. Mix the steak and kidney together. Put the flour and seasoning on a plate and use to coat the meat. To line a basin with the pastry, cut off ¼ of the dough and reserve for the lid. Roll out the rest of the pastry into a large, thin round. Lower into the basin. Add the meat and enough stock to come two-thirds of the way up the basin. Roll out the pastry for lid and place in position. Seal the edges. Cover with either greaseproof paper or foil, or a muslin cloth dipped in boiled water and then floured. Fix securely round the basin rim with string. Put the pudding in a steamer, stand this over a saucepan of boiling water and steam for 4 hours. Add more boiling water when necessary. Serve with creamed potatoes and Brussels sprouts.
Serves four.

Breast of Lamb and Onion Stuffing

675g (1½lb) breast of lamb, boned
15ml (1 tblsp) oil
15g (½oz) butter
Salt and pepper
Lamb seasoning
150ml (¼ pint) chicken stock
15ml (1 tblsp) cornflour, blended in a little cold water

Stuffing
30ml (2 tblsp) long grain rice
15g (½oz) butter
2 onions, peeled and chopped
Salt and pepper
Pinch of mixed spice
2.5ml (½ tsp) lamb seasoning

First make the stuffing. Cook the rice in boiling, salted water, rinse and drain. Heat the butter and fry the onion. Mix the rice and onion together with the salt and pepper, mixed spice and the lamb seasoning. Spread the stuffing on the lamb, roll and tie. Brush with the oil and butter, season and sprinkle with lamb seasoning. Roast in the oven for 20 minutes at 200°C, 400°F, Gas Mark 6. Reduce the heat to 180°C, 350°F, Gas Mark 4. Pour the stock into the roasting pan and cover with foil. Cook for a further hour. Remove the meat from the pan and thicken the gravy with the cornflour to accompany the meat. Serve with roast potatoes, turnips and mixed vegetables.
Serves four.

Peppered Mackerel with Gooseberry Sauce

225g (8oz) mackerel fillets, washed
25g (1oz) flour
50ml (2 fl oz) oil
10ml (2 tsp) peppercorns

Marinade
45ml (3 tblsp) oil
Grated rind and juice of 1 lemon
15ml (1 tblsp) soy sauce
1 clove garlic, peeled and crushed
15ml (1 tblsp) wine vinegar
15g (1 tblsp) sugar

Gooseberry Sauce
225g (8oz) gooseberries, topped and tailed
1 apple, peeled, cored and diced
50g (2oz) sugar
Sprig of mint
300ml (½ pint) water
Pinch of salt
15g (½oz) arrowroot (optional)

To make the marinade, liquidise all the ingredients in a blender. Soak the fish fillets in the marinade for 15 minutes. Drain them and dry on kitchen paper, then dip them in the flour. Discard the marinade. Brush the fillets with the oil and place on a greased grill rack. Grill for 3 minutes on each side, then remove, and sprinkle with peppercorns. Arrange on a hot dish and keep warm. Place the gooseberries in a saucepan with the diced apple, sugar, mint and half the water. Boil for 8 minutes, then remove the mint. Work the gooseberry mixture in a blender or rub through a sieve to a purée. Add a pinch of salt. Reheat the purée in a saucepan and thicken, if liked, with the arrowroot mixed to a paste with a little cold water. Boil for 4 minutes until clear and thick. Serve the grilled mackerel with the gooseberry sauce. Serve with new potatoes and mushrooms.
Serves four.

Lamb Cobbler

50ml (2 fl oz) oil
1 onion, peeled and sliced
675g (1½lb) minced lamb
30ml (2 tblsp) flour
30ml (2 tblsp) tomato purée
300ml (½ pint) brown stock
Salt and pepper
Pinch of rosemary
5ml (1 tsp) dry mustard
30ml (2 tblsp) Worcestershire sauce

Topping
225g (8oz) self-raising flour
Pinch of salt
50g (2oz) butter
50ml (2 fl oz) water
15ml (1 tblsp) milk

Heat the oil in a pan and fry the onion until soft. Add the lamb and cook for 5 minutes. Stir in the flour and tomato purée and cook for 5 minutes. Then add the stock, seasoning, rosemary, mustard and Worcestershire sauce. Make the topping by sifting the flour and salt together, and rub in the butter. Add enough water to form a dough. Roll out the dough to ¼ inch thick. Cut into rounds to form small scones. Arrange the scones around the top of the dish. Brush the scones with milk. Bake in the oven for 30 minutes at 190°C, 375°F, Gas Mark 5, until the scones are browned. Serve with creamed potatoes and Brussels sprouts.
Serves four.

Peppered Mackerel with Gooseberry Sauce (top), Lamb Cobbler (centre right) and Breast of Lamb and Onion Stuffing (bottom).

Quick Meals

Sausage Rolls

Shortcrust Pastry
450g (1lb) plain flour
Pinch of salt
100g (4oz) lard
100g (4oz) margarine
50g (2oz) Parmesan cheese

Filling
Salt and pepper
100g (4oz) Cheddar cheese
450g (1lb) sausage meat
A little beaten egg and milk, beaten
    together to glaze the pastry

To make the pastry, sift the flour
and salt into a basin. Add the
Parmesan cheese and rub in the fat.
Mix with enough water to form a
dough. Roll out into two rectangles
30cm x 25cm (12"x10"). Cut each
rectangle in half lengthways. Mix
the salt and pepper and Cheddar
cheese into the sausage meat and
roll out with the hands into four
lengths the same as the pastry.
Place on the pastry. Brush the
edges of the pastry with water, fold
over and seal. Cut into 3" lengths
and mark the top with a knife.
Brush with the milk and egg
mixture. Place on a greased baking
tray in the oven for 20 minutes at
200°C, 400°F, Gas Mark 6. Serve
with chips and peas or a mixed
salad.

Fisherman's Pie

450g (1lb) white fish fillets, steamed
450g (1lb) mashed potato
25g (1oz) butter or margarine
50g (2oz) Cheddar cheese (optional)

Sauce
25g (1oz) butter
25g (1oz) flour
300ml (½ pint) milk
Pinch of salt
5ml (1 tsp) dried parsley

Flake the cooked fish and place in a
pie dish. Make the sauce. Heat the
butter gently, remove from the heat
and stir in the flour. Return to the
heat and cook gently for a few
minutes but do not let the 'roux'
brown. Remove from the heat and
blend in the milk, stirring well. Add
salt and parsley. Cover the fish

with the sauce, then spread
mashed potato over the top of the
fish. Dot with small pieces of butter
or margarine and sprinkle with
Cheddar cheese, if desired. Cook
in the oven for 25-30 minutes at
200°C, 400°F, Gas Mark 6.
Serves four.

Savoury Eggs

450g (1lb) minced beef
1 large onion, peeled and grated
25g (1oz) white breadcrumbs
15ml (1 tblsp) Worcestershire sauce
Salt and pepper
2 eggs, beaten
4 hard-boiled eggs, shelled
Dried breadcrumbs
Oil for deep frying

Mix together in a bowl the minced
beef, grated onion, breadcrumbs
and Worcestershire sauce. Season
and bind the mixture with one of
the eggs. Divide the mixture into

four portions and mould round
each of the hard-boiled eggs. Dip
the covered eggs in the rest of the
beaten egg then coat with
breadcrumbs. Heat the oil in a
deep fat fryer or deep frying pan.
When hot, fry the savoury eggs for
5-10 minutes, until crisp and
golden brown. Serve hot or cold
with a green or mixed salad.
Serves four.

Chicken Marengo

1 large roasted chicken
50g (2oz) butter
50g (2oz) flour
600ml (1 pint) chicken stock
30ml (2 tblsp) tomato purée
Salt and pepper
1 beef stock cube
Pinch of mixed herbs
20g (¾oz) butter or margarine
1 onion, peeled and chopped
100g (4oz) sliced mushrooms
15g (½oz) sugar

Skin and bone the cooked chicken
and cut the meat into small pieces.
Melt the butter in a pan, and stir in
the flour to make a roux. Allow to
cool. Add the chicken stock and
the tomato purée and bring to
simmering point, stirring
continuously. Add seasoning, beef
stock cubes and mixed herbs. Fry
the onions and mushrooms in the
butter or margarine. Place the
chicken, mushrooms and onions in
an ovenproof dish. Pour the sauce
over chicken mixture and fold
through. Cover and cook in the
oven for 15 minutes at 230°C,
450°F, Gas Mark 8. Serve with
sauté potatoes and runner beans.

Cornish Pasties

450g (1lb) rump steak or good
    stewing steak
2 potatoes, peeled
2 onions, peeled
2 small carrots, peeled
25g (1oz) frozen peas
Salt and pepper
Pinch of mixed herbs
45ml (3 tblsp) brown stock
A little milk and egg beaten together
    to glaze

Shortcrust Pastry
450g (1lb) flour
100g (4oz) margarine
100g (4oz) lard
Pinch of salt
65ml (2½ fl oz) water

First make the shortcrust pastry.
Sieve the flour and salt into a bowl.
Rub in the fat until it looks like
breadcrumbs and mix with enough
water to form a dough. Divide into
four and roll out into rounds. Cut
the meat, potatoes, onions and
carrots into cubes and mix with the

**This page: Sausage Rolls (top),
Chicken Marengo (left) and
Savoury Eggs (bottom right).**

**Facing page: Cornish Pasties
(top), Cheesy Pizza (centre
right) and Fisherman's Pie
(bottom left).**

peas. Add seasoning and the herbs, add the stock and spoon onto the pastry rounds. Brush the edges of the pastry with a little water, bring the edges together and seal. Lift the pasties onto a greased baking sheet and brush with the egg and milk mixture. Cook in the oven for 25 minutes at 220°C, 425°F, Gas Mark 7. Lower the heat to 180°C, 350°F, Gas Mark 4 for a further 25 minutes to cook the meat and the vegetables thoroughly. Serve with chips, mushrooms and peas.
Serves four.

Picnic Burgers

50g (2oz) butter or margarine
1 onion, peeled and chopped
25g (1oz) flour
150ml (¼ pint) stock
Salt and pepper
350g (12oz) minced meat, cooked
75g (3oz) white breadcrumbs
Pinch of mixed herbs
10ml (2 tsp) chopped fresh parsley
1 beaten egg
45ml (3 tblsp) dried breadcrumbs
50g (2oz) fat

Heat the butter or margarine and fry the onion until soft. Stir in the flour and cook for a few minutes, then gradually stir in the stock, bring to boil and cook until thickened. Add seasoning. Stir in the minced meat and the breadcrumbs. Add the mixed herbs and parsley. Allow the mixture to cool, then form into 8 flat cakes. Coat with beaten egg and breadcrumbs. Fry in hot fat until crisp and golden brown. Drain on paper towels. Serve hot between buttered rolls or with vegetables.
Serves four.

Welsh Rarebit

25g (1oz) butter
25g (1oz) flour
150ml (¼ pint) milk
5ml (1 tsp) made mustard
Salt and pepper
225g (8oz) cheese, grated
15ml (1 tblsp) Worcestershire sauce
4 large slices of buttered toast

Melt the butter in a saucepan, stir in the flour and cook for several minutes. Allow to cool. Gradually add the milk, bring to boil, stirring, and cook until thick and smooth. Add the mustard, seasoning, most

of the cheese and the Worcestershire sauce. Heat steadily, but do not boil, until the cheese has melted. Spread over hot, buttered toast and sprinkle with the remaining cheese. Brown under a hot grill. Serve hot with chips.
Serves four.

Scotch Eggs

4 hard-boiled eggs, shelled
450g (1lb) sausage meat
1 egg, beaten
50g (2oz) breadcrumbs
5ml (1 tsp) mixed herbs
15ml (1 tblsp) flour
Oil

Using floured hands, coat the eggs with the sausage meat. Brush with the beaten egg. Combine the breadcrumbs and the mixed herbs. Roll the eggs in the breadcrumb and herb mixture. Fry the eggs in moderately hot oil for 10 minutes. Remove the eggs from the oil and drain well. Serve with bird's nest potatoes.
Serves four.

Cheesy Pizza

Pizza Dough
2.5ml (½ tsp) caster sugar
65ml (2½ fl oz) warm water
5ml (1 tsp) dried yeast
100g (4oz) plain flour
Pinch of salt
15g (½oz) lard
10ml (2 tsp) oil

Topping
400g (14oz) can of tomatoes
50g (2oz) mushrooms, sliced
2 bacon rashers, rinded and chopped
2.5ml (½ tsp) dried marjoram
100g (4oz) Cheddar cheese, grated
Stuffed olives, sliced

Dissolve the sugar in the water and sprinkle with the yeast. Leave in a warm place until frothy. Sieve the flour and salt into a bowl and rub in the lard. Blend the yeast liquid and the oil with the flour until a dough is formed. Turn the dough onto a floured board and knead well. Return the dough to the bowl and cover until it has doubled in size. Knead the dough again. Use the dough to line a 9" pizza plate. Before it starts to rise, brush with oil and cover with the topping. Drain the tomatoes and break

them up with a fork. Spread over the dough and cover with mushrooms and bacon. Sprinkle with the majoram. Top with Cheddar cheese and olives. Leave the pizza for 15 minutes before baking. Cook in the oven for 25 minutes at 200°C, 400°F, Gas Mark 6. Serve with a salad.
Serves three-four.

Hamburgers and Tomatoes

450g (1lb) minced beef
50g (2oz) breadcrumbs
150ml (¼ pint) tomato ketchup
1 large onion, peeled and chopped
2.5ml (½ tsp) mixed herbs
2.5ml (½ tsp) dried parsley
5ml (1 tsp) Tabasco sauce
Salt and pepper

Put all the ingredients into a bowl and mix well together. Form into eight rounds and chill in the refrigerator for 2 hours. Cook on an oiled grill or fry in a little oil for 5 minutes on each side. Serve with creamed potatoes and beans.
Serves four.

Saucy Chump Chops

4 lamb chump chops
25g (1oz) seasoned flour
45ml (1½ fl oz) oil
3 onions, peeled and sliced
3 tomatoes, skinned, deseeded and chopped
Pinch of garlic salt
150ml (¼ pint) white wine
150ml (¼ pint) chicken stock
Salt and pepper
4 courgettes, sliced
450g (1lb) potatoes, peeled
300ml (½ pint) white sauce
75g (3oz) Cheddar cheese, grated
5ml (1 tsp) Parmesan cheese

Coat the lamb chops with the seasoned flour. Heat the oil and fry the chops until browned on both sides. Remove from the pan and place in the bottom of an ovenproof dish. In the same oil fry the onions, add the chopped tomatoes and garlic salt. Pour in the wine and stock, add seasoning and simmer for 10 minutes. Blanch the courgettes in boiling water for 3-4 minutes. Drain and scatter over the chops. Pour the tomato mixture over the top. Blanch the potatoes in boiling water for 5 minutes. Slice

and arrange them over the top of the tomato mixture. Heat the white sauce and stir in 50g (2oz) of the Cheddar cheese and all the Parmesan cheese. Blend and pour over the potatoes. Sprinkle with the remaining Cheddar cheese. Cook in the oven for 1 hour at 160°C, 325°F, Gas Mark 3.
Serves four.

Party Hamburgers

450g (1lb) minced beef
2 medium onions, peeled and grated
1 medium potato, peeled and grated
Pinch of mixed herbs
Salt and pepper
1 beaten egg
A little fat
Buns or slices of bread
Butter (optional)

To Garnish
Rings of raw onion
Slices of apple dipped in lemon juice
Olives
Glacé cherries
Chopped spring onions
Yogurt
Parsley

Mix together the minced beef, onion, potato, herbs and seasoning. Bind with the beaten egg. Form into 4 round or square hamburger shapes. Either fry in a little hot fat, turning carefully, for about 15 minutes, or cook on a well-greased tray in the centre of the oven for 25 minutes at 200°C, 400°F, Gas Mark 6. Toast the buns or bread, and butter if desired. Put the cooked hamburgers on the buns or toast and keep warm until required. Garnish with raw onion rings, slices of apple dipped in lemon juice, olives, glacé cherries on cocktail sticks, chopped spring onions, yogurt and parsley. Serve hot with vegetables or cut small to eat with fingers.
Serves four.

Facing page: Hamburgers and Tomatoes (top right), Scotch Eggs (centre left) and Saucy Chump Chops (bottom right).

Sausage and Tomato Quiche

225g (8oz) chipolata sausages
75g (3oz) Cheddar cheese, coarsely
  grated
2 tomatoes, skinned and sliced
2 eggs
200ml (⅓ pint) milk
Salt and pepper
2.5ml (½ tsp) dried basil

Shortcrust Pastry
175g (6oz) plain flour
Pinch of salt
100g (4oz) fat
30ml (2 tblsp) cold water

Make the shortcrust pastry. Sift the flour and salt into a bowl. Rub in the fat until it looks like breadcrumbs and add enough water to make a dough. Roll out and line a flan case or pie plate with the pastry. Prick the base and sides and bake blind in the oven for 20 minutes at 200°C, 400°F, Gas Mark 6. Fry or grill the sausages until lightly browned. Sprinkle the cheese over the base of the cooked pastry case. Arrange the cooked sausages in a wheel design, and put tomato slices in between the sausages. Beat the eggs, stir in the milk, add seasoning and the basil. Pour over the quiche filling. Reduce the oven temperature to 180°C, 350°F, Gas Mark 4 and cook for a further 30-35 minutes. Serve hot or cold, with rice or salad.
Serves four.

Beef Shapes

25g (1oz) fat
1 medium onion, peeled and chopped
225g (½lb) minced cooked beef
Salt and pepper
Fat for deep frying

Sauce
25g (1oz) butter or margarine
25g (1oz) flour
300ml (½ pint) stock

Coating
15g (½oz) flour
Salt and pepper
1 egg, beaten
Dried breadcrumbs

Garnish
Watercress
Tomatoes

Heat the fat in a small frying pan. Add the onion and beef, cook gently for about 3 minutes until the beef turns brown, stirring with a fork. Cook gently for 10 minutes, until the onion is tender. Drain off any liquid. To make the sauce, melt the butter or margarine in a saucepan, blend in the flour and cook for 2-3 minutes. Add the stock gradually, stirring all the time. Bring the sauce to the boil and cook for 3 minutes. Add the beef mixture and mix well. When cool enough to handle, divide the mixture into 8 portions. Roll in seasoned flour, dip in beaten egg and coat with breadcrumbs. Heat the fat in a deep fat frier or deep frying pan, and fry the shapes until golden brown. Drain on paper towels. Garnish with watercress and tomatoes. Serve hot with vegetables, or cold with a salad.
Serves four.

Boston Baked Beans

50g (12oz) dried haricot beans
Cold water
2 medium onions, peeled and thinly
  sliced
225-350g (8-12oz) fat salt pork cut
  into 2.5cm (1") cubes
30-60ml (2-4 tblsp) black treacle
10ml (2 tsp) dry mustard
5ml (1 tsp) salt
Pepper

Wash the beans, cover with cold water and soak overnight. Drain, reserving the liquid and making up to 300ml (½ pint). Fill an ovenproof dish with the beans, onion and pork. Heat and mix the liquid with the remaining ingredients, including plenty of pepper. Pour into the ovenproof dish and cover. Cook in the oven for 5-6 hours at 140°C, 257°F, Gas Mark 1 or for 4 hours at 150°C, 300°F, Gas Mark 2. Stir occasionally, and add more water if the beans start to dry out while cooking. Serve with boiled potatoes.
Serves four-six.

Pork Sausage Croûtes

12 pork sausages
3 bacon rashers
A little fat
2 dessert apples, peeled, cored and
  sliced
6 bread rounds
2 tomatoes, sliced
Parsley to garnish

Fry the sausages until golden brown, without using extra fat. When cooked, place in a warm dish and keep hot. De-rind and halve each bacon rasher and roll and secure with a cocktail stick. Fry in a little fat, or without fat, until crisp. Keep warm with the sausages. Fry the sliced apples in hot fat until golden brown on both sides. Toast the bread. Place the sausages on top of the bread, then add the apple rings and uncooked tomato. Garnish with parsley and arrange the bacon rolls round the dish. Serve with baked beans or creamed potatoes and with a green vegetable.
Serves four-six.

Fish Pasties

4 plaice fillets
Salt and pepper
A little lemon juice
50-100g (2-4oz) mushrooms, thinly
  sliced
1 egg, beaten
4 tomatoes to garnish

Rough Puff Pastry
225g (8oz) plain flour
Pinch of salt
100-175g (4-6oz) fat
5ml (1 tsp) lemon juice
120ml (4 fl oz) cold water

Make the rough puff pastry. Sieve the flour and salt into a bowl. Rub in the fat cut into small cubes. Mix the lemon juice with the water and mix into the flour to make a dough. Roll out the pastry, fold and roll again, three times in total. Finally, roll into a large, fairly thick square and divide into four quarters. Lay a plaice fillet crosswise on each piece, season, and sprinkle with lemon juice. Cover with sliced mushrooms, damp the pastry edges and fold over to form a triangle. Press together and trim. Brush with beaten egg and bake in the oven for about 10 minutes at 190-200°C, 375-400°F, Gas Mark 5-6, or until the pastry is risen. Reduce the heat slightly and cook until brown. Cut the tomatoes into halves, place in an oiled dish and bake in the oven for 5 minutes. Put the egg left over from glazing into a separate ovenproof dish and bake for about the same time. When set, chop and place a spoonful on each tomato half. Put the pasties on a hot dish to serve and garnish with tomatoes and egg.
Serves four.

Chicken Risotto (left), Sausage and Tomato Quiche (below) and Boston Baked Beans (bottom).

Potato and Scrambled Egg

450g (1lb) potato or
225g (8oz) instant mashed potato
A little milk
100g (4oz) butter
Salt and pepper
2 eggs
150ml (¼ pint) milk
50g (2oz) Cheddar cheese, grated
Pinch of dry mustard

Cook or prepare the potatoes and mash them with a little milk, half the butter and seasoning. Place the eggs, milk, cheese and mustard in a bowl with seasoning. Beat together. Melt the remaining butter in a small pan and add the egg mixture, stirring continuously until all the fat is absorbed. Stir in the potatoes and egg mixture and mix together. Spread onto a large, flat surface and cut into shapes using assorted cutters. Place the potato shapes on an oiled grill and place under a hot grill for 10 minutes, until browned. Serve with fresh or tinned tomatoes.
Serves four.

Savoury Sausage Tournedos

450g (1lb) stewing steak, minced
Salt and pepper
5ml (1 tsp) mixed herbs
1 large onion
1 beaten egg
50g (2oz) fat
450g (1lb) can of baked beans with pork sausages and tomato sauce
1 large cooking apple

Mix the stewing steak with seasoning and the herbs. Peel the onion and cut into four even slices. Remove the centres from the onion rings. Finely chop the centres and remainder of the onion. Add the chopped onion to the steak, and bind with beaten egg. Divide the mixture into 4 rounds (tournedos). Heat the fat and fry the tournedos gently for 8 minutes on each side. Remove to a serving dish and keep hot. Heat the beans and sausages in a saucepan. Peel and core the apple and cut into four slices. Cook gently in the frying pan with the onion rings until the onion is golden brown and crisp, and the apples are tender but not broken. Place an onion ring on the tournedos, then a layer of

baked beans and top with an apple ring. Place two sausages inside the apple ring. Add the remaining baked beans and serve with creamed potatoes.
Serves four.

Risotto with Chicken

2 small onions, peeled and chopped
50g (2oz) butter
425g (15oz) can of tomatoes
15ml (1 tblsp) tomato purée
350g (12oz) long grain rice
900ml (1½ pint) chicken stock
60ml (4 tblsp) Parmesan cheese
450 (1lb) cooked chicken, diced
100g (4oz) mushrooms, chopped
Pinch of cayenne pepper

Fry the onion in the butter, add the tomatoes and tomato purée, and cook for 5 minutes, stirring continuously. Add the rice. Heat

the stock to boiling point. Add the stock to the rice and tomato mixture, cover and cook for 10 minutes. Remove from the heat and add the Parmesan cheese, cooked chicken, mushrooms and cayenne pepper. Cook gently for another 15 minutes, until all the liquid is absorbed.
Serves four.

Potato Figures

450g (1lb) potatoes, peeled
A little milk
50g (2oz) butter
Salt and pepper

Cook the potatoes in boiling, salted water for 20 minutes or until cooked. Drain the potatoes, add a little milk, the butter and seasoning and mash thoroughly. Spread the potato onto a large, flat surface and

cut into shapes using assorted cutters. Place the potato shapes on a greased baking tray and cook in the oven for 20 minutes at 180°C, 350°F, Gas Mark 4. Serve with sausages and tinned spaghetti.

Fish Cakes

225g (8oz) potatoes, peeled and cut into even-sized pieces
100g (4oz) white fish fillets
225g (8oz) potatoes
15g (½oz) butter or margarine
Salt and pepper
Oil for frying
1 sprig of parsley, to garnish (optional)

Coating
Flour
1 egg, beaten
Dried breadcrumbs

Cook the potatoes in a pan and cover with cold water, adding a little salt. Boil for 25 minutes until cooked. Steam the fish for 15 minutes until cooked. Mash the cooked potato, flake the fish and add to the potatoes with the butter or margarine and seasoning. Divide the mixture into six and shape into round fish cakes. Coat each cake with flour, beaten egg and finally breadcrumbs. Heat the oil in a frying pan. Fry the fish cakes carefully, cooking them on each side. Drain well on paper towels. Serve on a shallow dish and garnish with a sprig of parsley if desired. Serve with boiled potatoes and peas.
Serves six.

This page: Savoury Sausage Tournedos (top), Fish Pasties (centre right) and Pork Sausage Croûtes (bottom left).

Facing page: Potato Figures (top), Fish Cakes (centre right) and Potato and Scrambled Egg (bottom left).

The Family Roast

Lamb

ROASTING TIME: 25 minutes per 450g (1lb) + 25 minutes, at 160°C, 325°F, Gas Mark 3.

Place in the centre of a preheated oven. If a covered roasting tin is used basting is not necessary, but if the joint is uncovered or pot-roasted, the meat should be basted every 20-30 minutes. The meat should be turned over, using 2 metal spoons, halfway through the cooking. Transfer the meat from the tin to a hot, flat dish large enough to allow for carving. Keep hot. As accompaniments: medium brown, thickened gravy, mint or cranberry sauce. Serve with new potatoes, peas, French or runner beans.

Veal

ROASTING TIME: 25 minutes per 450g (1lb) + 25 minutes at 160°C, 325°F, Gas Mark 3.

Place in the centre of a preheated oven. If a covered roasting tin is used basting is not necessary, but if the joint is uncovered or pot-roasted, the meat should be basted every 20-30 minutes. The meat should be turned over, using 2 metal spoons, halfway through cooking. Transfer the meat from the tin onto a large, flat carving dish. Keep hot. As accompaniments: medium brown, thickened gravy, veal forcemeat stuffing, squeeze of lemon, bacon rolls. Serve with green vegetables, onions, tomatoes, baked or boiled potatoes.

Turkey

ROASTING TIME: For a 2.75-3.5kg (6-8lb) turkey cook for 15 minutes at 200°C, 400°F, Gas Mark 6, then reduce temperature to 180°C, 350°F, Gas Mark 4 and allow 15 minutes per 450g (1lb) + 15 minutes.

If the bird is frozen it must be allowed to thaw out completely before cooking. Stuff the bird, sprinkle with salt and place in a roasting tin. Brush the bird with melted dripping, butter or oil. The bird may be wrapped in foil, but the cover should be removed for the last 20-30 minutes to brown the skin. If left unwrapped, the bird should be basted frequently. Transfer to a large carving dish when cooked. As accompaniments: sausages, chestnut, sausage meat or veal forcemeat stuffing, bacon rolls, cranberry or celery sauce, thickened gravy. Serve with roast, fried or boiled potatoes, onions, peas or Brussels sprouts.

This page: Turkey (top), Pork (centre right) and Lamb (bottom).

Facing page: Mutton (top), Steak (centre left), Veal (centre right) and Duck (bottom).

Beef

ROASTING TIME: 15 minutes per 450g (1lb) + 15 minutes, at 180°C, 350°F, Gas Mark 4.

Place in the centre of a preheated oven. If a covered roasting tin is used basting is not necessary, but if the joint is uncovered or pot-roasted, the meat should be basted every 20-30 minutes. The meat should be turned over, using 2 metal spoons, halfway through the cooking. Transfer the meat from the tin to a hot, flat dish large enough to allow for carving. Keep hot. As accompaniments: thin, dark brown gravy, Yorkshire pudding, horseradish sauce, roast parsnips. Serve with baked or boiled potatoes and any vegetable.

Baked Whole Gammon

ROASTING TIME: 30 minutes per 450g (1lb) + 30 minutes at 180°C, 350°F, Gas Mark 4.

Spread gammon with a little melted butter or margarine and wrap in foil. Place in a roasting tin in the centre of a preheated oven. Transfer the meat from the tin when cooked, remove the foil and put the gammon onto a large, flat carving dish. Keep hot. As accompaniments: dark brown, thin gravy, sage and onion stuffing, apple sauce. Serve with baked or boiled potatoes, cabbage, celery, Brussels sprouts or cauliflower.

Pork

ROASTING TIME: 30 minutes per 450g (1lb) + 30 minutes, at 180°C, 350°F, Gas Mark 4.

Place in the centre of a preheated oven. If a covered roasting tin is used basting is not necessary, but if the joint is uncovered or pot-roasted, the meat should be basted every 20-30 minutes. The meat should be turned over, using 2 metal spoons, halfway through the cooking. Transfer the meat from the tin to a hot, flat dish large enough to allow for carving. Keep hot. As accompaniments: dark brown, thin gravy, sage and onion stuffing, apple sauce. Serve with boiled potatoes, cabbage, cauliflower, celery, onion, spinach or Brussels sprouts.

Duck

ROASTING TIME: For a 1-1.5kg (2-3lb) duck cook for 15 minutes per 450g (1lb) + 15 minutes at 180-190°C, 350-375°F, Gas Mark 4-5.

If the bird is frozen it must be thawed out completely before cooking. Stuff the bird with sage and onion stuffing, and place in a roasting tin. Brush the bird with melted dripping, butter or oil. Duck must be well pricked all over the breast to allow the fat to run out and leave the breast skin crisp and succulent. Transfer to a large carving dish when cooked. As accompaniments: apple sauce; thin gravy, flavoured with orange juice if liked. Serve with roast potatoes, peas, carrots and any green vegetable.

Steak

Season steak before cooking. Steak can be grilled, fried or roasted until tender and cooked to one's liking. Serve with baked or boiled potatoes and any vegetable.

Mutton

ROASTING TIME: 25 minutes per 450g (1lb) + 25 minutes, at 160°C, 325°F, Gas Mark 3.

Place in the centre of a preheated oven. If a covered roasting tin is used basting is not necessary, but if the joint is uncovered or pot-roasted, the meat should be basted every 20-30 minutes. The meat should be turned over, using 2 metal spoons, halfway through the cooking. Transfer the meat from the tin onto a large, flat carving dish. Keep hot. As accompaniments: medium brown, thickened gravy, redcurrant, cranberry or mint sauce. Serve with baked or boiled potatoes and any vegetable.

Chicken

ROASTING TIME: 15 minutes per 450g (1lb) + 15 minutes at 200°C, 400°F, Gas Mark 6.

If the bird is frozen it must be allowed to thaw out completely before cooking. Stuff the bird, sprinkle with salt and place in a roasting tin. Brush the bird with melted dripping, butter or oil. The bird may be wrapped in foil, but the cover should be removed for the last 20-30 minutes to brown the skin. If left unwrapped, the bird should be basted frequently. Transfer the bird to a large carving dish. As accompaniments: veal forcemeat, bread sauce, bacon rolls and thin gravy. Serve with baked, fried or boiled new potatoes, and green vegetables.

Beef (top), Chicken (far left) and Baked Whole Gammon (left).

Vegetables

for about 15 minutes at 200-220°C, 400-425°F, Gas Mark 6-7, until brown and crisp on the edges. An alternative to duchesse potatoes is to make birds' nests. Pipe the potato into rings and cook the same as for duchesse potatoes. Fill with vegetables.

Baked Potatoes

Peel potatoes and cut out any eyes and green parts. Cut into slices. Melt fat in an ovenproof dish and place potatoes in the dish. Cook in the oven at 220°C, 425°F, Gas Mark 7 for about 1 hour. Serve as required.

Potato

Potatoes (boiled)
New potatoes

Scrub potatoes well, then scrape. Cook in salted water for 10-20 minutes according to size. Drain well, toss in butter and serve.

Creamed Potatoes

Peel potatoes and cut out any eyes and any green parts. Cook in salted water for 15-20 minutes. When cooked, drain well. Using a potato masher or a fork, mash the potatoes in a pan until smooth and free of lumps. To each pound of potatoes add 25g (1oz) butter, a little milk and seasoning. Beat the mixture until light and fluffy. Serve as required.

Sauté Potatoes

Peel potatoes and cut out eyes and any green parts. Cook in salted water until they are almost cooked, drain well and allow to cool slightly. Cut into slices. Fry the potato slices in hot fat, turning them until crisp and golden brown on both sides. Serve as required.

Duchesse Potatoes

450g (1lb) cooked potatoes
25g (1oz) butter
1-2 egg yolks, beaten
A little hot milk if the egg yolks are small
10ml (2 tsp) salt
Pinch of pepper
A little egg and water mixed together to glaze

Put the hot, cooked potato through a sieve. Melt the butter in a saucepan. Add the beaten egg yolks and hot milk, if used. Beat well and add seasoning. Allow to cool slightly. Put into a piping bag with a star vegetable nozzle. Pipe in crowns on to a greased baking sheet. Brush with egg and water glaze. Cook in the top of the oven

This page: Baked Potatoes (top left), Creamed Potatoes (centre right) and Sauté Potatoes (bottom).

Facing page: Boiled Potatoes (top left), Duchesse Potatoes (top right), Birdsnest Potatoes (centre) and Potato Croquettes (bottom).

Potato Croquettes

450g (1lb) cooked potato
25g (1oz) butter
A little milk
10ml (2 tsp) salt
Pepper to taste
1 beaten egg
Breadcrumbs

Mash the cooked potato with the butter and a little milk. Add seasoning and leave to cool. Divide the mixture into even-sized portions. Roll each portion into a ball, using a little flour on the hands to prevent sticking. Using a palette knife and the hand, shape the balls into cork shapes, with flat ends. Coat with beaten egg and breadcrumbs. Fry in deep, hot fat until golden.

Old Potatoes

Peel potatoes and cut out any eyes and any green parts. Cook in salted water for 15-20 minutes until soft. Drain well and serve.

Bubble and Squeak

675g (1½lb) potatoes, peeled
A little milk
Knob of butter
450g (1lb) green cabbage, trimmed
   and roughly chopped
1 small onion, peeled and chopped
Salt and pepper
1 egg

Cook the potatoes in salted water until soft. Drain and mash with a little milk and butter. Plunge the cabbage into boiling, salted water. Cook for 5 minutes, drain well and finely chop. Mix the potato and cabbage with the onion, add seasoning and the egg. Put the mixture in a frying pan and fry in a little fat until golden brown.

This page: Bubble and Squeak (top), Potatoes Normandie (centre) and Jacket Potatoes (bottom).

Facing page: Brussels Sprouts (top), Mushrooms (centre left) and Glazed Carrots (bottom right).

This page: Creamed Spinach (top left), Peas (fresh) (top right) and Runner Beans (bottom).

Facing page: Cauliflower Cheese.

Glazed Carrots

50g (2oz) butter
450g (1lb) young carrots, scraped
   and quartered lengthways
Salt and pepper
Pinch of sugar

Garnish
Knob of butter
Chopped fresh parsley

Melt the butter in a pan. Add the carrots, seasoning, sugar and enough water to cover. Cook slowly without a lid for about 15 minutes, until the carrots are soft and the water has evaporated, leaving the carrots with a slight glaze. Serve in a warm dish. Garnish with a knob of butter and chopped parsley.

Mushrooms

Baked
Remove the stalks and peel off the outer skin, beginning from the edge and pulling towards the centre. Place in an ovenproof dish with a little butter, and cook for 10-15 minutes in the oven at 180°C, 350°F, Gas Mark 4.

Grilled
Prepare the mushrooms as above. Put a knob of butter the size of a pea on each mushroom in the hollow where the stalk was attached. Cook under a medium grill for 7-10 minutes.

Fried
Prepare mushrooms as above. Fry in butter for about 7-10 minutes until tender.

Cauliflower Cheese

1 cauliflower, washed and trimmed
25g (1oz) butter
25g (1oz) flour
300ml (½ pint) milk
100g (4oz) Cheddar cheese, finely
   grated
Salt and pepper
25g (1oz) fresh white breadcrumbs

Cook the cauliflower in boiling, salted water for about 10 minutes. Drain and place in an ovenproof dish. Melt the butter in a pan, add the flour and cook for a few minutes. Allow to cool before gradually adding the milk. Bring to the boil. Stir in 75g (3oz) of the cheese and season well. Pour the sauce over the cauliflower. Mix the remaining cheese and breadcrumbs together and sprinkle over the top. Brown in the oven for 5-10 minutes at 200°C, 400°F, Gas Mark 6 and serve.

Runner Beans

Top, tail and remove any tough strings. Shred the beans finely. Cook in boiling, salted water for 10-20 minutes until tender. When cooked, drain. Toss in butter and serve.

Creamed Spinach

1.5kg (3lb) fresh spinach, washed
 and coarse stalks removed
25-50g (1-2oz) butter
45ml (3 tblsp) single cream
Salt and pepper
Pinch of powdered nutmeg

Put the washed spinach in a saucepan with a little water. Heat gently, turning the spinach occasionally. Bring to the boil and cook gently for 10-15 minutes until very soft. Drain thoroughly and pass through a sieve or use a blender. Add butter, cream, seasoning and nutmeg to the purée. Return to the pan and reheat. Serve in a warmed dish.

Jacket Potato

Scrub the potato until the skin is clean. Remove eyes and any discoloured parts. Prick the skin, (this prevents the potato from bursting in the oven). Brush over with oil. Place on a baking sheet in the middle of the oven. Cook for between 1-2 hours, according to size of potato, at 180-190°C, 350-375°F, Gas Mark 4-5, until tender.

Potatoes Normandie

40g (1½oz) butter
675g (1½lb) potatoes, peeled and
 thinly sliced
Salt and pepper
300ml (½ pint) milk

Use a little of the butter to grease an ovenproof dish. Layer the slices of potato in the dish, seasoning between each layer. Pour the milk over the potatoes. Dot the remaining butter over the top. Cook in the oven for 1-1½ hours at 180°C, 350°F, Gas Mark 4, until the potatoes are soft. Serve with roast beef, lamb or pork.

Peas (Fresh)

Shell the peas. Cook in boiling, salted water with 5ml (1 tsp) salt, 5ml (1 tsp) sugar and a sprig of mint, for 10-15 minutes. Remove the mint, strain well and serve.

Beetroot (Boiled)

Boil beetroot in a saucepan for 1-1½ hours. Do not damage the skin before cooking. The skin will peel off easily once the beetroot is cooked.

Braised Celery

25g (1oz) butter
2 medium-sized carrots, peeled and diced
8 sticks celery, scrubbed, trimmed and cut in half lengthways
300ml (½ pint) chicken stock
Salt and pepper
Chopped parsley to garnish

Heat the butter and fry the carrots for a few minutes. Add the celery and cook for a further 2 minutes. Place the vegetables in an ovenproof dish and pour on the stock. Season well. Cover and cook in the oven for about 1-1¼ hours at 180°C, 350°F, Gas Mark 4. Garnish with chopped parsley.

Spring Greens

Wash well. Shred finely before cooking in boiling, salted water for 10-15 minutes. When cooked, drain well. Toss in butter, if liked, and serve.

Leeks

675g (1½lb) fresh leeks, washed, trimmed and halved
Butter
Pepper

Cook the prepared leeks in boiling, salted water for 10 minutes. Drain and toss in butter and add pepper.

Roast Parsnips

450g (1lb) parsnips, peeled, quartered and sliced

Garnish
Chopped fresh parsley

Cook the prepared parsnips in boiling, salted water for about 5 minutes. Drain well. Place in the fat around the joint and cook for about 45 minutes. Garnish with chopped parsley.

Brussels Sprouts

Cut a cross in the stalks and remove the outer leaves. Cook in boiling, salted water for between 7-15 minutes. When cooked, drain, toss in butter and serve.

Corn on the Cob

Strip off the husks and remove the silky threads. Cook the corn on the cob in boiling water for about 10-15 minutes, adding a little salt at the end of the cooking time. When cooked, drain. Serve with melted butter.

Broccoli

Thoroughly wash the broccoli and remove any withered leaves. Cook in boiling, salted water for 25-30 minutes. When cooked, drain and serve as required.

This page: Leeks (top), Roast Parsnips (centre left), Boiled Beetroot (centre right) and Broccoli (bottom).

Facing page: Braised Celery (top left), Spring Greens (top right) and Corn on the Cob (bottom).

Meals with Salads

French Dressing

15g (½oz) sugar
1.25ml (¼ tsp) salt
1.25ml (¼ tsp) dry mustard
150ml (¼ pint) vinegar
300ml (½ pint) corn oil

Blend the sugar, salt and mustard with the vinegar. Gradually beat or whisk in the oil, a little at a time. Taste and adjust the seasoning if necessary. Pour the dressing into a screw-topped jar. Shake vigorously before using, as the oil and vinegar will separate if left to stand.

Cheese and Ham Pie

Packet white sauce mix
100g (4oz) cheese, grated
100g (4oz) cooked ham, finely
    chopped
A little milk or beaten egg

Shortcrust Pastry
225g (8oz) flour
100g (4oz) margarine or fat
1 tsp salt
30ml (2 tblsp) cold water

First make the pastry. Sieve the flour and salt together in a bowl. Cut the fat into pieces and rub into the flour until it looks like breadcrumbs. Add the water to make a dough. Roll out enough pastry to line a shallow pie dish or tin. Make up the white sauce mix as directed on the packet. Mix the cheese and ham with the sauce and pour into the lined pie dish or tin. Roll out the remaining pastry to make a lid for the pie. Place on top, seal, and brush the top with milk or beaten egg. Place in the oven at 230°C, 450°F, Gas Mark 8 for 15 minutes. Reduce the temperature to 180°C, 350°F, Gas Mark 4, until cooked. Serve with a mixed salad.

Chunky Herrings

6-8 rollmop herrings
450g (1lb) small new potatoes,
    cooked
Small piece of cucumber, diced
Cooked peas
Sage or parsley to garnish

Vinaigrette Dressing
90ml (6 tblsp) oil
45ml (3 tblsp) wine vinegar
1.25ml (¼ tsp) chopped fresh herbs,
    e.g. tarragon, chervil
4-5 capers, chopped
Salt and pepper
Pinch of dry mustard

Remove the herrings from their liquid, drain well. Arrange the herrings on a flat dish. Blend together all the ingredients for the vinaigrette dressing. Mix the potatoes, cucumber and peas and toss with the dressing. Put the mixture round the herrings and garnish with sage or chopped parsley. Serve with a mixed salad. Serves six.

Mushroom Salad

Salt and pepper
Pinch of dry English mustard
135ml (4½ fl oz) oil
45ml (3 tblsp) wine vinegar
15ml (1 tblsp) chopped fresh parsley
1 garlic clove, peeled and crushed
350g (12oz) button mushrooms,
  sliced

Put the salt, pepper, mustard, oil, vinegar, parsley and garlic into a screw-topped jar and shake well. Pour over the mushrooms in a bowl. Leave to stand for 1 hour then serve.

Egg and Cheese Flan (far left), Chunky Herrings (centre) and Cheese and Ham Pie (above).

Egg and Cheese Flan

100g (4oz) cheese, grated
2 eggs
150ml (¼ pint) milk
1.25ml (¼ tsp) mixed mustard

Shortcrust Pastry
225g (8oz) flour
5ml (1 tsp) salt
100g (4oz) margarine or fat
30ml (2 tblsp) cold water

Make the shortcrust pastry. Sieve the flour and salt together into a bowl. Add the fat cut into pieces and rub into the flour until it is like breadcrumbs. Add the water to make a dough. Roll out and use to line a flan tin. Prick the base. Sprinkle with the cheese. Whisk the eggs, add the milk and mustard. Pour the egg mixture over the cheese. Cook the flan in the oven for 15 minutes at 230°C, 450°F, Gas Mark 8. Reduce the temperature to 160°C, 325°F, Gas Mark 3 and cook for about 30 minutes or until the flan is cooked. Serve with a mixed salad.

Dressed Crab

1 large cooked crab
Parsley to garnish

Pull off all the crab claws and wipe the shell. Turn the crab on to its back and firmly pull the body from the main shell. Remove and discard the stomach bag which lies behind the head and grey feathered gills or 'fingers' as these must not be eaten. Take out all the meat with a skewer or small spoon, putting dark and white into separate basins, then crack the top of the shell and remove pieces so there is a flat cavity to fill. Scrub inside the shell thoroughly under cold water. Dry and brush with oil. Crack the claws and remove the meat, adding it to the light meat. Arrange dark and light meat alternately in the shell and garnish with parsley. Serve with a mixed salad.

Kidney Beans and Onion

Salt and pepper
Pinch of dry English mustard
2.5ml (½ tsp) dried basil
1 garlic clove, peeled and crushed
45ml (3 tblsp) olive or corn oil
15ml (1 tblsp) wine vinegar
1 small onion, peeled and sliced
400g (14oz) can of red kidney beans, drained
Chopped parsley to garnish

Combine the salt, pepper, mustard, basil, garlic, oil and vinegar in a screw-topped jar. Lay the onion rings on a plate and sprinkle with salt. Leave for 30 minutes. Drain and rinse in cold water. Place the beans in a bowl, add the onion and toss in the dressing. Garnish with the chopped parsley and serve.

This page: Apple and Nut Salad (top), Kidney Beans and Onion (centre right) and Mushroom Salad (bottom). Facing page: Dressed Crab (top), Chicken Legs in Breadcrumbs (centre left), Tuna and Mackerel Loaf (centre right) and Chicken and Tomato Salad (bottom).

Chicken Legs in Breadcrumbs

Chicken legs as required
1 egg, beaten
Dried breadcrumbs
75g (3oz) oil or fat

Coat the chicken legs with the beaten egg and breadcrumbs. Heat the oil or fat in a pan. Fry the chicken fairly quickly until brown all over, then lower heat and cook slowly to cook right through. When pierced with a skewer the juices should run clear. Drain on crumpled paper towels. Serve with fried tomatoes and mushrooms and a green salad or other cooked vegetables.

Cucumber and Tomato Salad

450g (1lb) tomatoes, chopped
½ cucumber, finely diced
30ml (2 tblsp) French dressing
Watercress to garnish

Toss the cucumber and tomato in the French dressing. Garnish with watercress.

Tuna and Mackerel Loaf

1kg (2lb) sandwich loaf, one day old, refrigerated for 24 hours
50g (2oz) powdered gelatine
300ml (½ pint) white sauce
150g (5oz) canned tuna, drained
225g (8oz) mackerel fillets, drained
100g (4oz) cooked potato, diced
50g (2oz) cooked peas
50g (2oz) French beans, diced
50g (2oz) sweet corn
50g (2oz) cooked red peppers, diced
12 capers
25g (1oz) gherkins, diced
25g (1oz) chopped onion
Salt and pepper
Pinch of cayenne pepper
Juice and grated rind of ½ lemon
150ml (¼ pint) mayonnaise

Cut the crust off the loaf at one end and reserve. With a long bread knife cut round inside the crust and remove the bread from the centre. Scoop out any remaining crumbs. Dissolve the gelatine in 100ml (4 fl oz) hot water. Bring the white sauce to the boil, add the gelatine and simmer gently for 10 minutes until thick. Blend the tuna and mackerel fillets to a smooth paste. Add the paste to the thickened sauce and blend well. Mix in the rest of the ingredients except the mayonnaise. Cool and then add the mayonnaise. Fill the crust shell with the mixture. Replace the reserved crust, stand the loaf on a plate, place in the refrigerator and leave overnight to set. Serve by cutting into slices with a bread knife dipped in hot water. This is ideal for picnics or served with a mixed salad.

Bean Salad

175g (6oz) can kidney beans, drained
400g (14oz) can sliced green beans, drained
1 small onion, peeled and chopped
1 stalk celery, peeled and chopped
45ml (3 tblsp) wine vinegar
15ml (1 tblsp) oil
Few drops of sugar substitute
Salt and pepper

Mix the beans, chopped onion and chopped celery together. Mix the vinegar, oil, sugar substitute and seasoning together. Pour over the salad and leave to marinate in the dressing for a few hours, stirring occasionally. Serve well chilled with cold, lean meat.

Pineapple, Cheese and Celery Salad

120g (4oz) pineapple pieces
120g (4oz) cheese, diced
¼ head of celery, coarsely sliced
Salad cream for dressing
Lettuce
Watercress to garnish

Drain the pineapple and cut into small cubes. Toss with the other ingredients. Serve on a bed of lettuce, garnished with watercress.

Rice Salad

100g (4oz) patna rice
75g (3oz) pineapple pieces
150g (5oz) sweet corn
2 radishes, finely sliced
¼ red pepper, cored, seeded and finely sliced
¼ green pepper, cored, seeded and finely sliced
French dressing
Watercress or cucumber slices to garnish

Boil the rice in salted water for 15 minutes. Drain well and cool. Drain the pineapple thoroughly and cut into small cubes. Mix all the ingredients together in a bowl and toss in French dressing. Garnish with watercress or slices of cucumber.

Prawn Salad

90ml (6 tblsp) thick mayonnaise
15ml (1 tblsp) tomato purée
30ml (2 tblsp) lemon juice
15ml (1 tblsp) Worcestershire sauce
5ml (1 tsp) grated lemon rind
5ml (1 tsp) grated onion
10ml (2 tsp) chopped fresh parsley
Salt and pepper
About 100g (4oz) prawns

Mix the mayonnaise, tomato purée, lemon juice, Worcestershire sauce, lemon rind, onion, parsley and seasoning together thoroughly. Leave for 4 hours before using. Check the flavour before mixing the prawns with the sauce. Serve with a mixed salad.

Apple and Nut Salad

Salt and pepper
Pinch of dry mustard
45ml (3 tblsp) corn or olive oil
15ml (1 tblsp) wine vinegar
3 red eating apples, peeled and cored
8 sticks of celery, scrubbed and chopped
50g (2oz) chopped peanuts
Chopped fresh parsley to garnish

Put salt, pepper, mustard, oil and vinegar into a screw-topped jar and shake well. Put the apples and celery in a bowl with the chopped nuts. Pour the dressing over the apples and celery and toss well. Spoon into a serving dish and garnish with chopped parsley.

Chicken and Tomato Salad

1 lettuce, washed and cut into small pieces
2 cooked chicken breasts, sliced or
100g (4oz) bought sliced chicken
2 tomatoes, peeled and quartered
50g (2oz) frozen sweet corn, cooked and cooled
50g (2oz) frozen French beans, cooked and cooled

French Dressing
Salt and pepper
Pinch of dry English mustard
45ml (3 tblsp) olive oil
15ml (1 tblsp) wine vinegar

Make a French dressing by shaking together the salt, pepper, mustard, oil and vinegar in a screw-top jar. Place the lettuce pieces in a salad bowl, add the tomato, sweet corn and beans. Toss with the French dressing. Serve the chicken with the salad.

Cucumber and Tomato Salad
(left), Rice Salad (below) and
Pineapple, Cheese and Celery
Salad (bottom).

Mix the ingredients thoroughly together in a large bowl and dress with the salad cream. Garnish with mustard and cress or watercress.

Pasta Salad

100g (4oz) spaghetti
Knob of butter
2 carrots, peeled and coarsely grated
25g (1oz) raisins
6 radishes, finely sliced
¼ green pepper, cored, seeded and
    finely sliced
¼ red pepper, cored, seeded and
    finely sliced
30ml (2 tblsp) French dressing
Watercress or mustard and cress to
    garnish

Boil the spaghetti in salted water for 10-15 minutes. Drain well, toss in the butter and leave to cool. Put all vegetables and raisins together in a bowl and mix well. Toss in the French dressing. Garnish with watercress or mustard and cress.

Winter Salami Risotto

225g (8oz) salami, thinly sliced
100-175g (4-6oz) liver sausage,
    garlic sausage and luncheon meat,
    thinly sliced
2 green peppers
1 red pepper
4 large, ripe tomatoes
100g (4oz) green beans, cooked
8 stuffed olives
100-150g (4-5oz) medium or long
    grain rice, cooked
45-60ml (3-4 tblsp) vinaigrette
    dressing

Chop some of the meats and roll the remainder. Chop most of the vegetables, leaving a few large pieces for garnish. Slice the stuffed olives. Blend the rice with the vinaigrette dressing, chopped meat, vegetables and olives and put in the bottom of a shallow dish. Top with the larger pieces of vegetables and rolls of meat. Serve with a green salad.

Spanish Pâté

225g (8oz) chicken livers, minced
450g (1lb) pig's liver, minced
225g (8oz) minced beef
550g (1¼lb) pork, minced
350g (12oz) bacon fat, minced
15ml (1 tblsp) salt
Pepper
5ml (1 tsp) ground mace
15ml (1 tblsp) fresh mixed herbs,
    chopped
25ml (1 fl oz) sherry
50ml (2 fl oz) brandy
3 garlic cloves, peeled and crushed
75g (3oz) stuffed green olives

Mix together all the ingredients, except the olives, until well blended. Divide the pâté mixture between two well-greased terrines or loaf tins, adding the olives throughout the pâté, at different levels. Cover with foil and put in a roasting tin containing 5cm (2″) water. Cook for 2 hours in the oven at 150°C, 300°F, Gas Mark 2. Leave to cool. Place the pâté in the refrigerater for 1-2 hours, then turn into a serving dish. Serve with a mixed salad.

Coleslaw

225g (8oz) Dutch cabbage, finely
    shredded
2 radishes, finely sliced
¼ cucumber, finely diced
1 stick celery, finely diced
¼ green pepper, cored, seeded and
    finely sliced
¼ red pepper, cored, seeded and
    finely sliced
1 apple, peeled and finely sliced
1 large carrot, peeled and coarsely
    grated
Mustard and cress or watercress
Salad cream for dressing

This page: Bean Salad (top right), Coleslaw (centre left) and Pasta Salad (bottom). Facing page: Winter Salami Risotto (top), Prawn Salad (centre left) and Spanish Pâté (bottom).

Meals without Meat

Macaroni Cheese

175g (6oz) quick cooking macaroni
1.75 litre (3 pints) water

Cheese Sauce
40g (1½oz) butter
40g (1½oz) flour
450ml (¾ pint) milk
Salt and pepper
100g (4oz) Cheddar cheese, grated

Topping
25-50g (1-2oz) Cheddar cheese,
  grated
25g (1oz) dried breadcrumbs

Garnish
1 tomato
Parsley

Boil the macaroni in salted water for about 7 minutes. Add a little pepper if desired. Melt the butter in a saucepan, stir in the flour and cook for 2 minutes. Cool. Gradually blend in the milk, bring to the boil and cook until thickened and smooth. Add seasoning, and the cheese. Strain the macaroni and blend with the sauce. Put into a 1.2 litre (2-pint) dish, top with the cheese and breadcrumbs and brown under a hot grill. Garnish with tomato and parsley.

Cheese and Potato Whirls

100g (¼lb) instant potato powder or
1lb of potatoes, cooked
25g (1oz) butter and a little milk, if
  using cooked potatoes
450g (1lb) grated cheese
1 egg
Salt and pepper
Mixed mustard
Egg, beaten to glaze

Rough Puff Pastry
225g (½lb) plain flour
2.5ml (½ tsp) salt
175g (6oz) margarine
10ml (2 tsp) wine vinegar or lemon
  juice
150ml (¼ pint) ice-cold water

First make the pastry. Sieve the flour and salt into a bowl. Cut margarine into 1cm (½″) dice. Toss through the flour. Add vinegar or lemon juice to the water. Add to the flour and mix to a soft dough.

Turn on to a floured board. Roll into a square. Fold the side edges to the middle, top and bottom to middle, then fold in half. Press gently together. Leave to rest in refrigerator for 15 minutes. Remove and roll the pastry once again into a square, fold the side edges to the middle, top and bottom to middle, then fold in half. Make the instant potato as directed on the tin or packet or mash the cooked potato with the butter and milk. Add the cheese, egg, seasoning and mustard. Roll the pastry into a square, spread with the cheese and potato mixture. Roll up as for a Swiss roll and brush with egg to glaze. Cut into the required number of slices and cook on a baking tray in the oven for 20-25 minutes at 230°C, 440°F, Gas Mark 8.

Cheese Crust Vegetable Pie

Cheese Pastry

175g (6oz) flour
Pinch of salt
100g (4oz) butter or margarine
75g (3oz) Cheddar cheese, grated
30-45ml (2-3 tblsp) cold water to
   mix

Filling

50g (2oz) butter
1 onion, peeled and sliced
200g (7oz) can sweet corn
3 carrots, peeled and sliced
50g (2oz) mushrooms, sliced
50g (2oz) packet of leek soup
2 sticks celery, scrubbed and sliced
Pepper
1 egg, beaten to glaze

Sift the flour and salt into a mixing bowl. Rub the butter or margarine into the flour and stir in the cheese. Bind together with the water. Melt the butter in a pan and fry the vegetables for a few minutes. Drain on paper towels. Make up the packet of leek soup as directed, but using only 600ml (1 pint) of water. Stir the vegetables into the leek soup, season with pepper and pour into a 900ml (1½ pint) pie dish. Roll out the pastry to top the pie. Trim and flute the edges. Use any leftover pastry to decorate the pie top. Brush with beaten egg. Cook in the oven for 15 minutes at 200°C, 400°F, Gas Mark 6. Reduce the heat to 180°C, 350°F, Gas Mark 4, and cook for a further 20 minutes. Serve with new potatoes.

**Cheese Crust Vegetable Pie
(top), Cheese and Potato Whirls
(far left) and Macaroni Cheese
(above left).**

Corn Quiche

Pastry
175g (6oz) plain flour
Pinch of salt
75g (3oz) fat
30ml (2 tblsp) water to mix

Filling
200g (7oz) can sweet corn
2 eggs, beaten
300ml (½ pint) milk
100-175g (4-6oz) cheese, grated
Salt and pepper

Garnish
Parsley
Tomato

Sieve the flour and salt into a bowl.
Cut the fat into pieces and rub in
to the flour until it looks like
breadcrumbs. Mix with enough
water to make a dough. Roll out
and use to line a flan ring. Drain
the sweet corn and mix with the
eggs. Add the milk, cheese and
seasoning. Pour into the pastry
case. Cook in a hot oven for 15
minutes at 220°C, 425°F, Gas
Mark 7. Reduce the heat to 190°C,
375°F, Gas Mark 5 and cook for a
further 10 minutes. Garnish with
parsley and wedges of tomato.
Serve hot or cold.

Cheese Crowns

600ml (1 pint) milk
100g (4oz) fine semolina
100g (4oz) Parmesan cheese
10ml (2 tsp) made mustard
15ml (1 tblsp) Worcestershire sauce
Dash of cayenne pepper
Lettuce to garnish

Coating
1 egg, beaten
75g (3oz) dried breadcrumbs
Fat for frying

Grease a sandwich tin and set
aside. Heat the milk to near boiling
point. Stir in the semolina, bring to
the boil and cook, stirring
vigorously, for 3-4 minutes.
Remove the pan from the heat, add
the remaining ingredients and pour
into the prepared sandwich tin.
When the mixture is cold, turn
onto a floured board, and divide
into 8 wedges. Brush with beaten
egg and coat with breadcrumbs.
Heat the fat, carefully add the
wedges and shallow fry on both
sides until crisp and golden brown.
Drain on paper towels. To serve,
stand on end, top with cutlet frills
and serve on a bed of lettuce.

Savoury Egg Pie

Pastry
175g (6oz) plain flour
Pinch of salt
75g (3oz) fat
25ml (1½ tblsp) water

Filling
1 onion, peeled and chopped
25g (1oz) fat
450ml (¾ pint) milk
50g (2oz) soft, white breadcrumbs
3 large eggs, beaten
Few drops of Worcestershire sauce
Salt and pepper
Watercress to garnish

Sieve the flour and salt into a bowl.
Cut the fat into pieces and rub in
to flour until it looks like
breadcrumbs. Mix with enough
water to make a dough. Roll out
the pastry and use to line a pie
plate. Flute the edges. Fry the
onion in the fat, and spread over
the pastry. Warm the milk, add the
breadcrumbs and eggs. Stir in the
Worcestershire sauce and
seasoning. Pour the mixture into
the pastry case. Cook in the oven
for about 20-25 minutes at 200°C,
400°F, Gas Mark 6, until the pastry
is crisp and the filling is set.
Garnish with watercress and serve
hot or cold with salad.

Cheese Loaf

225g (8oz) self-raising flour
Pinch of salt
Pinch of dry mustard
50g (2oz) margarine
75g (3oz) cheese, grated
1 egg
85ml (3 fl oz) milk

Grease a small loaf tin and line the
bottom with greaseproof paper.
Sieve the flour, salt and mustard
together and rub in the margarine.
Add the cheese. Beat the egg and
milk together and reserve a little to
brush the top. Pour the rest into
the dry ingredients and mix to a

Cheese Bread Pudding

4 large slices of buttered bread
100-175g (4-6oz) Cheddar cheese,
 grated
Salt and pepper
5ml (1 tsp) Worcestershire sauce
Pinch of dry mustard
2 eggs
450ml (¾ pint) milk

Cut the crusts off the bread and
cut each slice into 6 squares. Fill a
greased, 900ml (1½ pint) pie dish
with layers of bread, cheese,
seasoning, Worcestershire sauce
and mustard. Reserve a little
cheese. Beat together the eggs and
milk and pour over the layers.
Sprinkle the top with the reserved
cheese and cook in the oven for
40-45 minutes at 160°C, 325°F,
Gas Mark 3. Serve with potato
croquettes.

Cheese Hot Pot

500g (1¼lb) potatoes
175g (6oz) onions
175g (6oz) carrots
250g (9oz) grated cheese
Salt and pepper
150ml (5 fl oz) water
Chopped parsley to garnish

Peel the potatoes, onions and
carrots, and cut into thin slices. Put
in layers into a deep dish, with the
cheese and a little seasoning
between layers. Continue until all
the vegetables are used, finishing
with a layer of cheese. Pour the
water into the dish to moisten.
Cover with a greased lid and cook
in the oven for 30 minutes at
230°C, 450°F, Gas Mark 8. Reduce
to 190°C, 375°F, Gas Mark 5, and
cook for a further 1½ hours.
Remove the lid and allow to brown
for about 5 minutes. Garnish with
chopped parsley.

soft dough. Shape into a loaf and
put into the tin. Cook in the oven
on a shelf above the centre for
about 35 minutes at 200°C, 400°F,
Gas Mark 6, until well risen and
golden brown. Cool on a wire tray.
Serve, sliced and buttered, the
same day. If kept to the next day,
serve toasted and buttered.

Egg and Potato Omelette

50g (2oz) butter
2 small cooked potatoes, diced
4 eggs
2.5ml (½ tsp) salt
Pinch of pepper

Heat the butter in a frying or
omelette pan. Add the potatoes
and cook until golden. Beat the
eggs and season. Add the eggs to
the potato and cook quickly until
the mixture is set. Fold over and
serve at once. Serve with a green
vegetable.

Kedgeree Fish and Mushrooms

175g (6oz) cooked smoked haddock
1 hard-boiled egg, shelled
225g (8oz) cooked, long grain rice
Pinch of cayenne pepper

Pinch of salt
100g (4oz) mushrooms
A little butter
Chopped fresh parsley

Flake the fish coarsely with a fork.
Chop the egg white, sieve the yolk
and put the yolk to one side for
garnishing. Using a fork mix the
flaked fish, chopped egg white,
cooked rice and seasoning in a
saucepan over moderate heat until
hot. Cook the mushrooms in a
little butter. Pile the mixture into a
hot dish and garnish with chopped
parsley and sieved egg yolk. Serve
at once with the cooked
mushrooms.

**Facing page: Cheese Hot Pot
(top), Cheese Crowns (centre
left), Corn Quiche (centre right)
and Savoury Egg Pie (bottom).**

**This page: Kedgeree Fish and
Mushrooms (top), Cheese Bread
Pudding (centre left), Cheese
Loaf (centre right) and Egg and
Potato Omelette (bottom).**

Meals for Special Occasions

Remove from the oven, allow to cool in the tin for 30 minutes, then turn out and leave to cool completely. Drain the apricots, reserving the juice. Garnish the loaf with apricot halves and the stuffed olives. Mix the cornflour with a little of the apricot juice, then add the rest of the juice and the wine. Heat, stirring, until thickened. Cool, then brush over the meat loaf and serve the rest separately in a jug. Serve the meat loaf on a bed of lettuce leaves, with potato croquettes and vegetables. Serves eight-ten.

Boeuf en Croûte

15ml (1 tblsp) oil
1.5kg (3lb) beef topside
25g (1oz) butter
1 onion, peeled and chopped
100g (4oz) button mushrooms, chopped
30ml (2 tblsp) freshly chopped parsley
Salt and pepper
275g (10oz) bought or home-made rough puff pastry
A little milk
Few sprigs of watercress to garnish

Heat the oil in a large pan and fry the meat quickly on all sides to seal the juices. Transfer the oil and the meat to a roasting dish. Cook in the oven for 45 minutes at 200°C, 400°F, Gas Mark 6. Leave to cool. Melt the butter in a pan and fry the onions until soft. Add the mushrooms, parsley and seasoning. Cover and fry for 5 minutes. Roll out the pastry to make a rectangle large enough to cover the meat. Spread ⅓ of the stuffing over the

Turkey and Apricot Loaf

675g (1½lb) uncooked turkey meat, minced
175g (6oz) fresh white breadcrumbs
1 onion, peeled and finely chopped
15ml (1 tblsp) Worcestershire sauce
1 egg, beaten
Pinch of mixed herbs
Pinch of allspice
Salt and pepper
425g (15oz) can apricot halves
100g (4oz) stuffed, green olives, sliced
10ml (2 tsp) cornflour
150ml (¼ pint) dry white wine

Grease a 450g (1lb) loaf tin and set aside. In a large bowl, mix together the turkey, breadcrumbs, onion, Worcestershire sauce, egg, herbs, allspice and seasoning, and combine well. Spoon the mixture into the loaf tin, making sure the corners are well filled, smooth over the top and bang the tin on a flat surface to release any air bubbles. Cook in the oven for about 90 minutes at 180°C, 350°F, Gas Mark 4, or until the meat loaf is cooked through. The juices will run clear when a skewer is inserted.

This page: Sweet and Spicy Noisettes (top), Veal in Orange (centre left) and Peppered Steak (bottom right).

Facing Page: Boeuf en Croûte (top), Turkey and Apricot Loaf (centre left) and Stuffed Trout with Almonds (bottom).

centre of the pastry and place the meat on top. Spread the rest of the stuffing over the meat. Dampen the edges of the pastry and fold them over the meat like a parcel. Trim as necessary. Place the meat, joins downwards, in a roasting pan. Roll out any pastry trimmings and cut into leaf shapes, to decorate the top. Brush the top with a little milk. Increase the oven temperature to 220°C, 425°F, Gas Mark 7, and cook the beef for about 40-45 minutes until the pastry is golden. Place the meat on a serving dish and garnish with watercress. Serve with baked potatoes, Brussels sprouts and carrots.
Serves six-eight.

Veal in Orange

750g-1kg (1½-2lb) veal fillet
1 onion
600ml (1 pint) white stock
Salt and pepper
2 oranges
4 small, young carrots
225g (8oz) long grain rice
50g (2oz) butter
40g (1½oz) flour
Pinch of powdered saffron
150ml (¼ pint) double cream
Parsley to garnish

Dice the veal. Peel the onion and keep it whole. Put the veal, onion, stock and seasoning into a pan. Bring to the boil. Lower the heat and simmer for 40 minutes until the meat is tender. Remove the onion. Cut away the peel from 1 orange, remove the white pith, then cut the orange flesh into narrow strips. Soak in 150ml (¼ pint) water for 30 minutes. Peel the carrots, cut into neat matchsticks, put with the orange rind and a little seasoning and simmer in a covered pan for 20 minutes. Remove the carrots and orange rind and cook the rice in remaining salted water. Heat the butter in a pan, stir in the flour and cook for several minutes. Add the strained veal stock and bring to the boil. Cook until thickened. Add the orange rind, carrots, cooked rice and any liquid left, together with the pinch of saffron powder and the cream. Stir over a low heat until smooth. Add the cooked veal and mix thoroughly. Arrange a border of rice with the remaining orange cut into slices on a serving dish. Spoon the veal mixture in the centre of the dish and sprinkle with parsley. Serve with potatoes and vegetables of your own choice.
Serves six.

Veal with Cucumber

225-350g (8-12oz) fillet veal, cubed
Salt and pepper
15ml (1 tblsp) cornflour
50g (2oz) butter
100g (4oz) button mushrooms
2 eating apples, peeled, cored and sliced
1 cucumber, peeled and diced
1 green pepper, cored, deseeded and sliced
1 red pepper, cored, deseeded and sliced
100g (4oz) cooked rice

Sweet and Sour Sauce
15ml (1 tblsp) cornflour
30ml (2 tblsp) sugar
10ml (2 tsp) soy sauce
45ml (3 tblsp) vinegar
150ml (¼ pint) chicken stock

Toss the veal in seasoned cornflour and fry in the butter until golden. Remove and keep warm. Fry the mushrooms, apple slices and cucumber. Fry the peppers. Return the meat to the pan. Cover and cook for 10 minutes until the meat is tender. Stir in the cooked rice. Transfer to a serving dish and keep hot. Mix the sweet and sour sauce ingredients together, add to the pan and, stirring gently, boil for 2-3 minutes, until the sauce is transparent. Pour the sauce over the veal and cucumber mixture. This can be served as a meal in its own right, or served with a vegetable if required.
Serves four.

Sweet and Spicy Noisettes

5ml (1 tsp) honey
5ml (1 tsp) dry mustard
Salt and pepper
1 garlic clove, peeled and crushed
10ml (2 tsp) lemon juice
6 noisettes of lamb
3 canned pineapple rings with juice
15g (1oz) butter
20ml (1½ tblsp) chopped mint
1 tomato, quartered
3 glacé cherries

Combine the honey, mustard, seasoning, garlic and lemon juice and spread the noisettes with the mixture. Leave to stand for 20 minutes. Place 50ml (2 fl oz) of the pineapple juice in a pan, add the butter and bring to the boil. Boil until reduced by half and add the mint. Keep warm. Grill the noisettes, basting them occasionally with the pineapple mixture. When the meat is cooked, arrange it on a warmed serving dish and decorate with the tomatoes and the pineapple rings. Garnish with the glacé cherries. Serve with fried mushroom rings and bird's nest potatoes.
Serves three.

Stuffed Trout with Almonds

Salt and pepper
2 medium trout, filleted
100-150g (4-5oz) butter
50g (2oz) blanched almonds

Stuffing
175g (6oz) fresh, white breadcrumbs
30ml (2 tblsp) chopped fresh parsley
1 medium onion, peeled and finely chopped
Salt and pepper
10ml (2 tsp) mixed dried herbs
1 cooking apple, peeled and finely chopped
1 small egg, beaten
A little water

Season the fish lightly and fry for about 10 minutes in the butter, until tender. Transfer to a hot dish. For the stuffing mix together the breadcrumbs, parsley, onion, seasoning, herbs and apple. Stir in the beaten egg, and water if necessary, to give a soft consistency. Stuff the fish with this mixture. Fry the almonds for about 5 minutes, adding extra butter if necessary. Scatter the almonds over the fish. Garnish with parsley, and serve with sauté potatoes and a vegetable.

Three Ring Rice

1 red pepper
100g (4oz) butter or margarine
225g (8oz) cooked rice
2 medium onions, peeled and chopped
½ green pepper, cored, deseeded and chopped
1 small garlic clove, peeled and crushed
225g (8oz) minced beef
175g (6oz) can of concentrated tomato purée
5ml (1 tsp) salt
2.5ml (½ tsp) chilli powder
100g (4oz) packet of frozen peas

Core, deseed and cut the red pepper into strips. Arrange at intervals in the bottom of a ring mould. Melt half the butter or margarine. Stir in the rice and spoon into the mould over the pepper. Fry the onion and green pepper together with the garlic in the remaining butter until soft. Add the minced beef and cook until brown. Stir in the tomato purée, salt and chilli powder. Cook the peas, strain, put on top of the rice, then cover with the beef mixture. Press down each layer firmly. Place the mould in a shallow pan of hot water. Cook in the oven for about 20 minutes at 180°C, 350°F, Gas Mark 4, or until firm to the touch. Turn out onto a hot dish. Serve with sweet corn or a side salad.

Veal with Cucumber (above right) and Three Ring Rice (below right).

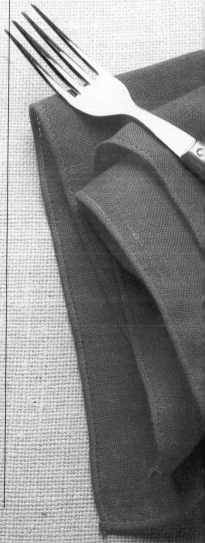

layers. Season each layer and add herbs. Pour over the juice from the tomatoes and finish with a layer of potato slices. Pour water in to come halfway up the dish and dot the butter over the top. Cover tightly and cook in oven for 90 minutes at 180°C, 350°F, Gas Mark 4. Remove the lid and cook for a further 30 minutes to brown the potatoes. Serve with boiled carrots tossed in butter and chopped parsley.
Serves six.

Gammon with Mixed Fruit

1.75-2.25kg (4-5lb) gammon hock
30ml (2 tblsp) apricot jam
30ml (2 tblsp) made mustard
Cloves for decoration
1 small, fresh pineapple, peeled
15ml (1 tblsp) chutney
60ml (2¼ fl oz) unsweetened pineapple juice
1kg (2lb) canned apricot halves, drained

Cover the gammon with cold water and soak for 4 hours. Drain the gammon and wrap in foil. Place in a roasting pan and cook in the oven for 2 hours at 190°C, 375°F, Gas Mark 5. Remove the rind from the gammon and score the surface of the meat. Mix half the apricot jam with the mustard and spread the mixture over the gammon. Stud the meat with the cloves in a decorative pattern and return the meat to the oven for about 30 minutes. Cut the pineapple into slices and remove the core from each slice. Heat the remaining apricot jam with the chutney and pineapple juice in a wide pan. Glaze the pineapple slices and the apricot halves in this mixture. Place the finished gammon joint in a serving dish and garnish with the glazed pineapple slices and apricot halves. Serve with an exotic salad.
Serves ten.

Crown Roast of Lamb

2 best ends of lamb, chined
10ml (2 tsp) butter
1 cooking apple, peeled, cored and chopped
225g (8oz) pork sausage meat
30ml (2 tblsp) fresh breadcrumbs
15ml (1 tblsp) chopped fresh parsley
15ml (1 tblsp) finely chopped mint
Glacé cherries

Trim the skin and fat from the ends of the rib bones so that 2.5cm (1 inch) of the bone protrudes. Place the two joints back-to-back with the bones curving upwards and outwards. Secure with kitchen thread. Heat the butter and sauté the apple, add the sausage meat, cook for 2-3 minutes then stir in the rest of the ingredients. Place the stuffing in the cavity of the crown. Cover the tips of the bones with foil and roast in the oven for 30 minutes per 450g (1lb) plus 30 minutes at 180°C, 350°F, Gas Mark 4. Decorate the bone ends with cutlet frills and glacé cherries and serve with roast potatoes and a green vegetable.
Serves six-eight.

Pork Provençal

1kg (2lb) pork fillets
425g (15oz) can tomatoes
750g (1½lb) potatoes, peeled and thinly sliced
350g (12oz) onions, peeled and thinly sliced
Salt and pepper
1.25ml (¼ tsp) dried mixed herbs
25g (1oz) butter

Slice the meat and trim off any surplus fat. Butter an ovenproof dish then arrange the tomatoes, meat, onions and potatoes in

This page: Pork Provençal (top) and Turkey Roast with Fruit Sauce (bottom).

Facing page: Crown Roast of Lamb (top), Egg and Melon Salad (bottom left) and Gammon with Mixed Fruit (bottom right).

Egg and Melon Salad

1 small cabbage
1 firm, ripe melon
1 orange
Salt and pepper
2 carrots, peeled and grated
4 hard-boiled eggs
Few sprigs of watercress
Few leaves of chicory
8 radishes

Cooked Salad Dressing
5ml (1 tsp) flour
15ml (1 tblsp) sugar
Salt and pepper
2.5ml (½ tsp) mustard powder
1 large egg, beaten
30ml (2 tblsp) water
30ml (2 tblsp) vinegar
5ml (1 tsp) butter

To prepare the dressing, combine the flour, sugar, mustard and seasoning in a heavy-based saucepan. Mix in the egg to form a smooth paste. Add the water, vinegar and butter and stir over a low heat until the sauce begins to thicken. Remove from the heat, stir thoroughly and, if necessary, strain to remove any lumps. Cool in the refrigerator. Chop the cabbage very finely. Cube the melon. Peel the orange and cut the segments into pieces. Combine these ingredients with the grated carrots in a mixing bowl. Season as required. Pour over the cooled dressing and spoon the salad mixture onto a large salad dish. Shell and slice the hard-boiled eggs and arrange them with the watercress and chicory leaves round the salad. Cut the radishes into floral shapes and garnish the salad and serve.
Serves four.

Barbados Turkey

25g (1oz) flour
5ml (1 tsp) powdered ginger
5ml (1 tsp) curry powder
100g (4oz) turkey escalopes
75g (3oz) butter
50ml (2 fl oz) rum
50g (2oz) desiccated coconut
45ml (3 tblsp) pineapple juice
70ml (2½ fl oz) chicken stock
50ml (2 fl oz) double cream
Salt and pepper
Few sprigs of parsley
6-8 slices canned pineapple

Mix together the flour, ginger and curry powder and use to coat the turkey. Heat the butter and fry the escalopes for about 10 minutes each side until cooked and golden. Add the rum and set alight. When the flames subside, remove the

escalopes and keep hot. Add the coconut to the pan and brown quickly. Then stir in the pineapple juice and stock. Boil for 5 minutes, reduce the heat and stir in the cream and seasoning. Arrange the escalopes in a serving dish and cover with the sauce. Garnish with the parsley and pineapple. Serve with boiled rice and green vegetables.
Serves four.

Crown of Chicken

Salt and pepper
25g (1oz) flour
1kg (2lb) potatoes
45ml (3 tblsp) milk
25-50g (1-2oz) butter
6 or 8 chicken legs
60ml (4 tblsp) olive oil
1 can cherry fruit pie filling
Watercress to garnish

Coat the chicken legs in seasoned flour. Peel the potatoes and cook in boiling, salted water. Drain and mash the potatoes with the milk and butter and keep hot. Meanwhile, fry the chicken in the olive oil until cooked and golden brown. Drain on paper towels and keep hot. Drain excess oil from the frying pan, add the cherry pie filling and heat gently. Place the creamed potatoes in centre of a hot serving dish, stand the chicken legs round the edges. Pour over the hot cherry sauce. Garnish with watercress and serve with a green salad.

Duck with Orange Sauce

1 large duck, e.g. 1.5kg (3lb)
1 orange
300ml (½ pint) bought Espagnole sauce
15ml (1 tblsp) lemon juice
30ml (2 tblsp) white wine
150ml (¼ pint) water
Orange segments to garnish

Place the duck in an open roasting tin. No fat is necessary. Cook in the oven at 150°C, 300°F, Gas Mark 2. Cook for 25 minutes for every 450g (1lb) in weight and 30 minutes over. Prick the breast skin after 30 minutes with a fine skewer. Pare the rind from the orange, cut into wafer-thin strips and simmer in water for about 10 minutes. Strain the Espagnole sauce carefully, reheat with the orange rind, orange juice, lemon juice and wine. Garnish the duck with orange segments and serve with

the orange sauce. Serve with potato croquettes, broccoli and roast turnips.
Serves four.

Peppered Steak

Steak, as required
A little oil or butter
Peppercorns

Brush the steak with oil or melted butter and grill until tender, or as required. When the steak is cooked, place on a serving dish and sprinkle with the peppercorns. Tap with a steak hammer to crush the peppercorns into the steak. Serve with French fries, potato croquettes, onion rings or broccoli, or a mixed side salad.

Turkey Roast with Fruit Sauce

25g (1oz) butter
2.5kg (5½lb) white turkey roast
1 red pepper
1 small green pepper
1 onion
225g (8oz) can mandarin oranges
225g (8oz) canned sweet corn

For the Sauce
10ml (2 tsp) cornflour
15ml (1 tblsp) vinegar
5ml (1 tsp) sugar
5ml (1 tsp) Worcestershire sauce
15-30ml (1-2 tblsp) sherry

Spread the butter over the turkey roast then wrap in foil to make a parcel. Place in a roasting pan and roast in the oven for 90 minutes at 190°C, 375°F, Gas Mark 5. Core, deseed and chop the peppers. Peel and chop the onion. Drain the mandarins and sweet corn, reserving the juices. Mix the mandarins, sweet corn, peppers and onion together. To make the sauce, mix the cornflour with a little water to make a smooth paste. Blend the juices from the mandarins and sweet corn with the vinegar, sugar, Worcestershire sauce, sherry and cornflour and heat until thickened, stirring well. Add the fruit and vegetables. Remove the turkey roast from the

oven and unwrap the foil. Pour a little of the sauce all over and round the turkey and cover again with the foil. Cook the turkey for a further 1-1½ hours or until the turkey is tender and cooked through. Unwrap the turkey and place on a serving dish. Surround with fruit sauce and serve the rest of the sauce separately. Serve with roast potatoes and vegetables of your own choice.
Serves six-eight.

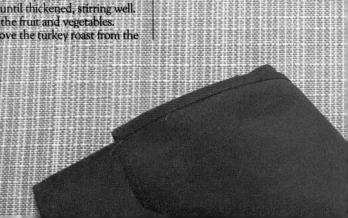

Crown of Chicken (right),
Duck and Orange Sauce
(below) and Barbados
Turkey (bottom).

Index

Apple and Nut Salad 48
Bacon and Chestnuts 10
Baked Potatoes 36
Baked Whole Gammon 35
Barbados Turkey 62
Bean Salad 48
Beef 35
Beef Bake 15
Beef and Dumplings 19
Beef Shapes 28
Beef Surprise 15
Beetroot (boiled) 42
Black Pudding with Apple 20
Boeuf en Croûte 56
Boiled Potato 36
Boston Baked Beans 28
Braised Beef 8
Braised Celery 42
Breast of Lamb and Onion Stuffing 22
Broccoli 42
Brussels Sprouts 42
Bubble and Squeak 38
Cauliflower Cheese 40
Cheese Bread Pudding 55
Cheese Crowns 54
Cheese Crust Vegetable Pie 53
Cheese and Ham Pie 44
Cheese Hot Pot 55
Cheese Loaf 54
Cheese and Potato Whirls 52
Cheesy Pizza 26
Chicken 35
Chicken Casserole 16
Chicken Curry 8
Chicken Legs in Breadcrumbs 48
Chicken Marengo 24
Chicken Pie 15
Chicken and Tomato Salad 48
Chunky Herrings 44
Cod in White Sauce 15
Coleslaw 50
Corn on the Cob 42
Corn Quiche 54
Cornish Pasties 24

Country Chicken 18
Creamed Potatoes 36
Creamed Spinach 41
Crown of Chicken 62
Crown Roast of Lamb 60
Crunchy Lamb Pie 20
Cucumber and Tomato Salad 48
Demi-Glacé Sauce 10
Dressed Crab 46
Duchesse Potatoes 36
Duck 35
Duck and Orange Sauce 62
Egg and Cheese Flan 46
Egg and Melon Salad 62
Egg and Potato Omelette 55
Filled Jacket Potatoes 12
Fish Cakes 30
Fish Pasties 28
Fisherman's Pie 24
French Dressing 44
Gammon with Mixed Fruit 60
Gammon Rounds in Onion Sauce 20
Glazed Carrots 40
Hamburgers and Tomatoes 26
Hearts and Stuffing 12
Jacket Potato 41
Kedgeree Fish and Mushrooms 55
Kidney Beans and Onion 46
Lamb 32
Lamb Cobbler 22
Lasagne 12
Leeks 42
Liver with Oranges 18
Macaroni Cheese 52
Meat Loaf 20
Mixed Grill 8
Mushroom Salad 45
Mushrooms 40
Mutton 35
Old Potatoes 38
Party Hamburgers 26
Pasta Fish Pie 8
Pasta Salad 50
Peas (fresh) 41
Peppered Mackerel with Gooseberry
    Sauce 22
Peppered Steak 62
Picnic Burgers 26
Pineapple, Cheese and Celery Salad 48
Plaited Lamb 8

Pork 35
Pork Chops with Brussels Sprouts and
    Sweet Corn 16
Pork Fillets and Apricots 10
Pork Provençal 60
Pork Sausage Croûtes 28
Potato Croquettes 38
Potato Figures 30
Potato Normandie 41
Potato and Scrambled Egg 30
Poussin in White Sauce 7
Prawn Salad 48
Rice Salad 48
Risotto with Chicken 30
Roast Parsnips 42
Runner Beans 40
Saucy Chump Chops 26
Sausage Rolls 24
Sausage and Mushroom Pie 12
Sausage and Tomato Quiche 28
Sauté Potatoes 36
Savoury Egg Pie 54
Savoury Eggs 24
Savoury Sausage Tournedos 30
Scotch Eggs 26
Shepherd's Pie 16
Smoked Haddock in French Mustard
    Sauce 7
Spaghette Bolognese 15
Spanish Pâté 50
Spring Greens 42
Steak and Kidney Pudding 22
Stuffed Aubergines 12
Stuffed Mushrooms 8
Stuffed Trout with Almonds 58
Sweet and Sour Pork Chops with Rice 15
Sweet and Spicy Noisettes 58
Three Ring Rice 58
Toad in the Hole 20
Tuna and Mackerel Loaf 48
Turkey 32
Turkey and Apricot Loaf 56
Turkey Roast with Fruit Sauce 62
Veal 32
Veal with Cucumber 58
Veal Cutlets Bonne Femme 8
Veal in Orange 58
Welsh Rarebit 26
Wine Coated Ham 20
Winter Salami Risotto 50